Blind Landing

Blind Landing

Bjørn Konow Paulsson

Translated from the Norwegian
by Constance Ford Toverud

Harcourt Brace Jovanovich, Inc.
New York

Originally published in 1968 in Norway by H. Aschehoug & Co. under

the title of *Blindlanding*

ISBN 0-15-208770-2

Library of Congress Catalog Card Number: 77-161388

Printed in the United States of America

First American edition

B C D E F G H I J

Contents

1   Squadron 666   7

2   Training, Training, Training   32

3   Forced Landing   40

4   Navigational Flying   55

5   Norwegian National Championship   69

Chapter 1

Squadron 666

Sergeant Tore Bö straightened his tie and adjusted the cap of his uniform with a slightly unsteady hand. He was nervous—or perhaps "keyed up" was a better way to put it—and filled with excited anticipation of all the new experiences awaiting him. He sat in the rear of the bus that would take him to Gardermoen Air Base and his new squadron, 666.

He still wasn't quite sure why he had chosen that particular squadron. Upon completion of their jet training at Rygge, the pilots had been given a form to complete with their requests for future assignments.

Tore was the only one who had chosen 666. It had been recently formed, using the F-86-K, a type of aircraft that had run into a lot of snags in the Air Force. Trouble always seemed to follow a new type of aircraft —trouble for both the pilots and the ground crew—and the F-86-K had been involved in many fatalities.

Tore had always been reserved and a bit reluctant to call attention to himself. At the same time, everything new and unknown held a certain fascination for him.

The fact that several sergeants had lost their lives in the plane didn't concern him unduly. If one thought about the risks involved in flying jets—crashes, fires, parachute ejections—one might as well quit flying.

The bus stopped, and the driver turned to the young sergeant.

"We're here. Take that road to the right about a hundred yards and you'll find the gate."

"Thanks a lot." Tore grasped the bag the driver handed him and jumped down the last step.

His back erect, his blond hair visible beneath the cap of his uniform, he resembled any sergeant returning from leave. But on the right side of his chest shimmered silver-gray wings—the insignia of a pilot. He couldn't help glancing at them occasionally. He was still so new and eager that he was stirred with pride each time he saw them.

The scream of brakes startled him out of his thoughts, and he turned abruptly.

"Scare you?" A laughing face peered out of the window of the jeep.

"Uh—no," answered Tore, wondering what it was all about. He looked more closely at the boy whose face was one big grin. Then he saw the single star on his shoulder. The rest of his uniform revealed that he was a pilot—a second lieutenant.

"Want a lift? Looks like we're going the same way." The lieutenant opened the car door so Tore could toss in his bag.

"Thanks. I'd appreciate that."

Tore climbed in beside the lieutenant, who stepped on the gas so hard that the tires whined.

"Rough driving," thought Tore, and glanced at him.

"My name's Arild Nansen," said the lieutenant.

"I'm Tore Bö."

"Where are you heading?" asked Arild.

"I'm not sure, but I'm joining 666."

"How about that! You must be our new sergeant." Arild took one hand from the wheel and stretched it out toward Tore. "Welcome!"

"Do you fly with 666, too?" Tore liked this friendly, direct fellow.

"You bet I do. B Wing, that's me." Arild laughed. "There are so few of us in the squadron right now that I'm alone on B Wing for the time being. The squadron chief promised me the first new one that came. Must be you."

Tore liked the idea of flying with Arild. Of course he would fly with older, more experienced pilots first in order to be checked out on this particular aircraft, but he'd be in close touch with Arild since they would be in the same wing.

Arild drew up at the gate and was waved through by the guard. The 30 m.p.h. speed limit posted on a sign by the road didn't seem to bother Arild, and he sped along at 60 m.p.h. The jeep tilted as he rounded a corner on two wheels. Arild chuckled. "Nothing more fun than driving a jeep," he explained. Tore wondered if he flew the same way he drove a car—too fast and with too little control in the turns. Well, he'd find out soon enough.

More sharp turns and then Arild stopped suddenly with a screeching of brakes in front of a large red building.

"The squadron's hole-in-the-wall. Come on in and meet the boys!"

Arild sprang out of the jeep. Tore had a little trouble collecting his long legs.

Arild waited impatiently for Tore by the door. He opened it quickly and almost shoved Tore in ahead.

"Hi, gang, look what I found—a brand-new sergeant for my wing. Meet Tore Bö, imported directly from Rygge."

Five pilots were sitting around a table. One was reading a magazine. One sat tipped backward in a chair, his feet on the table. Two of them were eagerly studying a map spread out on the table in front of them. The fifth man held an oxygen mask in his lap and was adjusting something on it.

Each one looked up and stared curiously at the newcomer. Tore reddened slightly. For a moment no one said anything. Tore realized they were taking stock of him. What if he didn't measure up? The boys looked very tough. He noticed that all held the rank of lieutenant. Perhaps they had forgotten how it felt to be introduced to a new squadron as a sergeant.

The lieutenant holding the oxygen mask rose and came over to him.

"Welcome. It's always a pleasure to see a fresh new face. These sourpusses"—he gestured toward the others —"can get on your nerves."

The other four began to laugh, and the ice was broken.

"I'm Peter Knutsen. The one with the long snout is Finn Karlsen, the little guy is Per Lund, the feet on the table belong to Sigurd Sivertsen, and the last one, the squadron's laziest, stupidest, and nicest lieutenant, is named Stein Larsen."

The introduction had been made in a light and straightforward manner. Tore liked it and already felt almost accepted. One by one the boys came forward to shake hands.

"Where's the major?" asked Arild.

"He's up with Hans," answered Knutsen. "Hans had a little accident yesterday, you know, when he landed a bit too short. The major wanted to check out his approach procedure personally."

"Well, have a seat, Tore. We'll meet the major when he comes down." Arild pointed to two empty chairs by the table.

The other men resumed their discussion, and Tore listened closely. He liked listening to others, to anything anyone had to say as long as it made sense. In this way he was able to pick up a lot of useful tips. Arild soon joined the conversation, and Tore realized that his new friend was quite a different person when he talked about flying. He was quiet, thoughtful, and knowledgeable; occasionally excitable, perhaps, but never angry.

The discussion was suddenly interrupted by a deafening noise overhead. Tore jumped slightly.

"That was the major coming in low," explained Arild. The others only glanced out of the window and saw that the major was flying at a permissible altitude.

Arild told Tore that it was usual to buzz the building at the completion of such a flight, but naturally it depended both on the air traffic and the weather. Ten minutes later they heard the familiar whine of an approaching jet. It was the major and Hans taxiing in to the hangar.

Tore looked out of the window and saw how precisely and elegantly the two pilots swung into place at the mechanic's signals. Then the whine died away, and it was quiet again.

The door opened and in walked a tall, dark man in full flying togs. He threw his helmet and chute into a corner, loosened the zipper in the tight-fitting G suit, took off his gloves, and slumped into a chair beside Tore.

He had been greeted by a "Hi, Major," from the others, so there was no doubt as to his identity. He looked tired, but it was always like that after a flight.

One hour in the air with maneuvers and plenty of G effect was the equivalent of five hours of logging in the north woods.

Tore sat quiet and attentive. Before long the major turned to say something and noticed Tore's expectant and somewhat shy expression.

"Oh, you must be Bö." The major extended his hand. Tore rose.

"Sit down, sit down—and stay sitting. In this flight we aren't very formal, and we don't stand at attention when addressed by a superior. Welcome to the group. You've met the others and are ready to get started?" The major glanced at the clock. "Fourteen hundred hours ought to be all right, or would you prefer to take it easy today?"

"No, Major, I'd really like to fly right away." Tore had an empty feeling in his stomach at the thought of climbing into an unfamiliar plane. All jets are pretty much alike in terms of equipment, instruments, checklists for takeoff, flying, and landing. But each type has to be handled in a special way and has its own reaction pattern—just as a Volkswagen is different from a Mercedes.

"Knutsen, will you take the flight and make sure that Bö gets well acquainted with the K?"

"OK, Major."

"Well, good luck, Bö!" He got up, nodded to the others, and disappeared into the next room.

"We'll go over in the corner here." Knutsen pointed to a little booth used for flight briefings. The wall was covered with drawings, maps, orders to be followed, and a large survey map of Gardermoen and vicinity.

For more than an hour, quiet voices were audible from the corner—one steady and instructive, the other eagerly questioning. Tore followed closely everything Knutsen said, absorbing each word and trying to remember it all.

After a while Knutsen asked some questions to determine how much Tore had understood. He was satisfied with the answers and thought to himself that the new sergeant was quick on the uptake.

"There—that's enough for now. We'll grab some lunch and work with the aircraft itself afterward."

Tore was ready for a break. His head was full of new knowledge, important minor rules, various speed limits, temperatures, and checks.

He wasn't particularly hungry and thought only about the coming flight. The uneasy feeling in his stomach would not go away, and he was glad when lunch was over and he was on his way back to the squadron again with Knutsen.

Without exchanging a word they donned their flight suits. Tore had sent his from Rygge earlier in the week, and it hung in its place in the hall locker in the squadron building. He attached the oxygen mask to the test plug in the wall to see if it functioned normally. He tightened the straps slightly. Everything was in order.

"Let's go." Knutsen disappeared through the door,

and Tore had to break into a jog to catch up with him. The parachute slung over his shoulder was heavy, so his progress was slow.

Tore had been assigned to the plane with the letter X for X-ray.

The K was bigger and heavier than the F-86-F, which Tore had flown previously at Rygge, and the engine was more powerful. In addition, the K had an afterburner. He had never flown with an afterburner before and anxiously wondered about its effect. He'd heard plenty of stories about it, particularly about its defects that affected the plane's forward thrust. The stories were often frightening, but Tore had no time to think about them now. He was far too busy checking to see if all panels were fastened, all screws tightened, and if the movable parts went in the directions they were supposed to.

The mechanic, Sergeant Gunnar Lie, followed Tore's movements closely and made occasional comments as they walked around the plane.

"X-ray is the best plane in the squadron," he said. "It's never had any major defects, so you can feel plenty secure." The last remark was intended as a slight comfort to the pilot about to make his first flight in the new type of aircraft.

Tore looked over to the plane beside his in which Knutsen had already settled himself in the cockpit and was waiting.

Tore strapped on his parachute and tightened the

straps securely; one never knew when one might have use for it. Lie helped him into the cockpit and bent over him to fasten the harness and remove the safety pins from the ejection seat.

The instruments glared blankly at Tore, but they would soon come to life. Tore fastened his helmet, adjusted the seat to the correct height, and attached the oxygen mask to the cylinder. He stole a glance at Knutsen, who waved and pointed to his ears. Tore flipped the radio switch and immediately heard a low hum. He checked to see if the channel selector was tuned to the correct frequency. It was.

"Can you read me, Yellow 2?" That was Knutsen's voice. It came through high and clear in Tore's ear.

"Yes. Loud and clear."

"Take plenty of time before you fire up, and go through the checklists very carefully! I'll wait until you've finished."

"Roger," answered Tore.

He settled himself more comfortably in the seat and pulled out the thick checklist with all the items to be gone through before he would be ready for takeoff. He followed the list exactly, examining each item minutely, and everything appeared to be in order.

He was ready for takeoff. Lie stood directly in front of the left wing and waited for the all-clear signal for ignition. His hand rested on the external power unit, which would give the plane's batteries additional power to rotate the starting engine.

Tore flipped on the necessary switches and pointed his left thumb straight up. Lie pushed the button. Tore waited. A low howl began, gradually increasing in intensity. Several indicators on the instrument panel began to dance back and forth. Tore kept an eye on all of them.

The plane shuddered slightly, and the vibrations increased. The engine instruments told Tore that the engine had started. Rapidly he turned on several more switches and nodded to Lie, who unplugged the external unit and ran under the wings to drag away the wheel chocks. Next he pulled the external unit away and signaled with the thumbs-up sign to Tore. All clear! Tore was on his own.

The instruments had settled down and now lay within the green arc that indicated the correct readings. If they showed red, there was danger.

Tore read the checklist again and made the necessary adjustments. The queasiness in his stomach was gone. He was far too busy carrying out the procedures to offer a thought to anything else.

"Yellow 2 from Yellow 1, are you all set?"

"Roger, Yellow 1." Tore glanced at Knutsen, who was holding up his thumb.

"Gardermoen tower, Yellow 1 and 2—taxi instructions. Over."

"Roger, Yellow. Runway 02, wind 360 degrees at 05 knots. You're ready for takeoff position. Over."

"Roger," replied Knutsen.

According to their agreement Tore would taxi out first. Knutsen would position himself on Tore's wing to keep tabs on what was happening.

Tore shoved the throttle forward, and the engine

roared. As the plane began to move forward, he stepped on the right-hand brake and swerved onto the runway. In the overhead mirror he saw Knutsen directly behind him.

Only now did Tore realize that he was about to fly. Still on the ground, yes, but the noise of the engine and the plane's movements felt great. He looked up at the sparkling blue sky and pulled down the visor so he wouldn't be blinded by the sun.

Still more checks were completed on the way down the runway. Everything worked as it should.

Tore reached the runway and swung the plane to the right of the median line to make room for Knutsen on the other side.

He applied the brakes. It was time for the engine check. For the first time he would use the afterburner. Now he *had* to hold the plane quiet while he read the indicators.

He waited until Knutsen had taken his position beside him, slightly behind the left wing of the plane.

"Yellow 1 and 2, you are cleared for takeoff when you are ready." It was the tower clearing them.

"Roger, Yellow 2, get going." Knutsen's voice sounded encouraging.

The next minutes were always the most critical of the entire takeoff procedure. If the engine power failed when needed, the consequences were catastrophic. It's not exactly a pleasure when a plane tears off a runway at several hundred miles per hour.

The thought of engine failure occurred to Tore, but

18

it always did just before he was airborne. The uneasiness in his stomach returned.

He looked at Knutsen, who nodded. Tore let his left hand glide slowly forward, while simultaneously he stood on the brakes. The angry roar from the motor increased rapidly, and the plane vibrated more and more as Tore gave it the gas. Now he had reached 90 percent. A violent shaking began as the afterburner cut in. The needle on the tachometer rose to 100 percent. A tremendous surge of power tore through the plane—power waiting to be released.

All instruments gave the proper indications, as stable as they were supposed to be. Tore drew back the throttle to idling position. The needle fell rapidly. Right. Everything OK.

Knutsen had carried out the same checks. Everything normal there, too.

"Well, we might as well take the jump," thought Tore. He looked at Knutsen again, gave the thumbs-up sign, and received an immediate answer.

Tore's hand shook a tiny bit as he placed it on the throttle to push it all the way forward.

Knutsen kept his eyes riveted on him, for a nod from Tore meant that the brakes had been released and the plane would begin to roll forward at full speed.

Tore nodded as he released the brakes and was pressed back into his seat. It was just as if someone had given him a good kick.

The plane eased forward, and the speed increased.

Tore concentrated on holding the plane straight on the runway and simultaneously fastened his eyes on the instrument panel. The engine instruments indicated that the afterburner was 100 percent effective, the temperature normal. The air-speed indicator moved slowly around.

Now Tore raised the nose of the plane by drawing slightly back on the stick, slowly and easily. No abrupt movements now. The critical moments were at hand as he lifted the plane off the ground. If the engine failed, he would have to set down hard, and he had already used up too much of the runway to be able to stop before reaching the end of it at his present speed. All this rushed through his thoughts as he pulled gently on the stick and felt the plane straining to lift its nose higher as the wheels hopped lightly along the ground. The hopping ceased, and he was in the air. The earth disappeared rapidly beneath him. There was the edge of the runway! The altimeter began rotating —100 feet, 200 feet. He reached for the landing gear handle and pulled it up, sensing the slight bang and lurch of the plane as the wheels snapped into place in the wheel wells. Then up came the flaps and the plane was clean, as they say in flying jargon.

This was Tore's first opportunity to look about for Knutsen, and a glance to the side startled him. He was looking straight into the cockpit at him. Knutsen had followed Tore the entire way and was very pleased with the assured maneuvers.

"Yellow 1 from tower. You are cleared on course. Good trip!"

"Roger. Yellow 2, we are setting a northerly course and will climb to 20,000 feet. Over."

"Roger," replied Tore. He was thrilled with the sensation of air under his wings again.

In the cockpit it was quiet as a tomb. The noise of the engine in a jet flows behind it, so there is no racket in the cockpit. All that could be heard was the quiet whisper caused by wind resistance, the air as it was pressed past the body of the plane, and the slight buzz of the radio in his earphones. Tore swung a little to the left and looked down. Gardermoen grew smaller and smaller beneath him. The contours on the ground became clearly visible. People, animals, cars, and houses were still discernible, but in miniature. The roads wound around like snakes and made tracks through the landscape, which appeared increasingly flat.

Tore had drawn back the throttle from the forward position and had cut out the afterburner. He no longer needed it as he went into an even climb. In fact, he would have little use for the afterburner from now on —only if something had to happen fast and he had to increase speed or climbing ability.

Knutsen had moved a bit more to the side and lazily followed Tore up. He had only to follow Tore's movements and watch that they were executed correctly, noting possible errors, which would be discussed after the men came down. Tore himself determined the pattern. It was a flight designed for the pilot to become familiar with the plane. Later there would be more demanding maneuvers—aerobatics, dives, and more.

Even though it was a routine flight, Tore sweated inside his flight suit. Concentration was just as necessary in straight flying as it was playing loop-the-loop. He angled the plane into gently climbing turns and felt how lightly the plane reacted—how it responded to each touch on the stick. He felt increasingly at one with the K. It was a terrific plane. And what ascent power! It wasn't long before the altimeter indicated 19,000 feet, and he had to think about leveling off in order not to exceed his designated altitude. Knutsen had said 20,000 feet, and he meant 20,000 feet, not 20,100. Everything had to be precise in the air. An error of only one hundred feet could mean catastrophe in certain situations. You had to train for precision right from the beginning. This was emphatically stressed during pilot training, even before the first flight.

Tore pushed the stick way forward, throttled back a little to the desired r.p.m., trimmed the elevators, and the plane continued forward at exactly 20,000 feet.

Knutsen noted on his pad: level-off good.

Knutsen and Tore had agreed on the course to be followed, so there was no radio communication between them. Radio silence is another important rule. Radio discipline, as it is called. No unnecessary talk in the air.

Knutsen adjusted his position and came up on Tore's right, a little to the side. He relaxed. This was going fine.

Tore pulled the map from his side pocket and spread it out on his knee. He must become familiar with the terrain over which they were flying, locate typical landmarks to which he might refer later. From this altitude he had a superb view. Behind him lay Oslo and the Oslo Fjord. Lake Mjösa lay under him, just to the right was Hamar, and in the distance, beyond the plane's nose, he could see the village of Lillehammer.

Over Lillehammer they were to turn west.

While he compared the map with the ground, he swept the instrument panel constantly with his eyes, carefully noting if he were maintaining the correct speed, altitude, and course. Everything had to be exact. A light touch on the stick turned the plane a few degrees to the west. There! Now he was on course again.

They were to stay up one hour, and Tore was amazed when he saw the clock. Had time really passed that quickly?

The two planes had passed Fagernes and turned their noses south again.

"Yellow 1 from Yellow 2—I'll take over now. I'm approaching from your right."

"Roger," answered Tore. He glanced to his right and watched Knutsen glide up and past. The plane sparkled in the sun. Tore was proud to be sitting in such a beautiful aircraft.

"Position yourself fifty feet directly behind. I'll do a few little maneuvers. Hang on as well as you can." Knutsen sounded in high spirits.

Tore reduced his air speed and slipped neatly into

the indicated position. He lowered the seat a notch and tightened the safety belts. No more straight flying. He looked over the instrument panel and checked to see that he had switched off the radio compass, the artificial horizon, and the other instruments which might be damaged by abrupt changes in direction.

Knutsen began with a few easy turns, which gradually became sharper until the plane lay at a ninety-degree angle.

Suddenly he leveled the aircraft and aimed the nose downward, increasing the speed. Tore waited with eyes glued to the exhaust cone ahead of him. The tiniest movement from the plane ahead had to be imitated instantaneously. It would be pretty embarrassing to lose contact with the lead plane.

It was a joyous game in the air. But there was a serious purpose behind the maneuvers. Knutsen was testing Tore's reaction speed and flying ability, and at the same time Tore was learning what the plane could do and the way it handled in unfamiliar positions and situations.

The plane changed position; almost unnoticeably the tail sank down and the nose began to point upward. Tore pulled carefully on the stick and felt himself being pressed down into the seat. The blood drained from his brain because of the sudden change in body weight, and there was a flickering before his eyes.

This was the familiar G effect so deeply respected by every pilot. It could be dangerous, causing unconsciousness if powerful enough. When a plane suddenly changes direction at high speed, the body—and particularly the blood—are subject to considerable changes in pressure. It is similar to the centrifugal force affecting a car in a sharp curve.

Tore had pulled so gently on the stick that the flickering disappeared almost at once. It wasn't the first time that Tore had experienced the G effect, but he didn't like it—the unpleasant awareness that for a moment one was not in full control of oneself.

Knutsen's plane continued straight upward, and Tore began to wonder if it would ever change direction.

Suddenly the sky was in the wrong place. Tore was staring straight up toward a large lake. The plane lay on its back; he hung in his straps and saw Knutsen's plane beneath him. Knutsen was on the way down again, and Tore had been so attentive that he had been able to follow the slightest movement.

The planes flew straight down in a tremendous dive. Tore knew he had plenty of altitude, but the earth seemed to be approaching at an incredible speed. The sky was back where it belonged, and he sat comfortably in his seat. He heard the wind howling outside, which told him that the plane's speed was steadily increasing. How far down would Knutsen go? Could Tore pull out of the dive correctly this time without too many G's?

He checked the speedometer and the other instruments—just a quick glance. If he looked at them too long, the plane in front might alter direction in the meantime.

Knutsen's plane indicated a more moderate diving angle, and Tore was suddenly watchful. Gently back on the stick, just a little at a time! The plane reacted willingly—the wild dive became more and more gradual, until finally the nose of the plane pointed once more in a climb. Tore felt no unpleasant G effects. Recovery from the dive had been well coordinated and correct.

Tore rejoiced. He had executed his first loop with the K, and it had been done perfectly.

"Good work, Yellow 2." The voice was Knutsen's. He had watched Tore carefully in the mirror and registered the care and precision reflected in the performance of the plane behind him.

Pride welled up in Tore, and he began a jarringly off-key song that only he could hear. He had to smile —he was acting like a kid! But there was something special about flying this way—danger from one moment to the next, suddenly lying upside down and gazing at Mother Earth—the whole time in complete control of the plane, which obeyed his slightest command. He was an absolute monarch in infinite space.

For ten minutes they flew across a wide expanse of sky. To anyone standing on the ground, they would be seen only as two white streaks executing mystical figures. Strange indeed to the uninitiated.

"Time to get back." Knutsen's voice sounded in Tore's ear. Homeward, sure. . . . Tore had completely forgotten to observe their position. He had been too busy following the plane in front of him. That was a real "goof." A pilot should always know his position at any given moment, whether lying on his back or not.

The map had slid to the floor, and Tore peered out to sight a definite landmark. But beneath him were only fields, tiny ponds, and a train track that wound through the landscape—but in which direction?

"You can take over, Yellow 2, and fly back to the base."

"Roger." Tore couldn't very well say that he didn't know in which direction Gardermoen lay. Or could he? No, he'd take his chances.

Knutsen had glided out to the side, and Tore drew back on the throttle. At the same time he switched on the radio compass and the gyro. When the instruments had settled down, he saw that they were flying in a westerly direction. That had to be wrong. Quickly he swung the plane to the south. They had been to the west of Mjösa when they began the maneuver. He could only hope that he was on the right track. In the meantime, he'd better check the map for definite landmarks. He bent over quickly and picked up the map. Each pond and lake looked like all the others, no typical identifying characteristics. He wondered if he ought to swing a bit eastward. No, he'd wait a little longer.

Directly ahead of the plane appeared a larger body of water with a curious formation—it reminded him of a carrot. A quick look at the map and he found it. He was sixty degrees off course. Gardermoen lay in a southeasterly direction. Slowly he adjusted the plane to the approximate course he had chosen. A rapid calculation of the speed told him he had about ten minutes left.

After five minutes' flying he clearly saw Lake Hurdal, and there was Gardermoen! Ten degrees to the left, and his course was correct.

"OK, Yellow 2, you finally found it. I'll take over now." Was Knutsen's voice amused? Or was it annoyed? Tore regretted having indicated his uncertainty.

"Gardermoen, Yellow 1 and 2 in for landing."

"Roger, Yellow 1. Runway 02 in use, wind calm, call up three miles out."

"Roger, Yellow 1. Runway 02 in use, wind calm, call up three miles out."

Knutsen confirmed. "Yellow 2, extend speed brakes . . . now."

Tore extended his speed brakes so the speed decreased and they could drop to the desired altitude. Simultaneously he pushed the throttle in slightly.

During the rapid descent the altimeter whirled around. When they had reached 3,000 feet, Knutsen carefully flattened out and reduced speed. At 1,500 feet he flew straight ahead. That was the height at which they were to circle for landing.

"Gardermoen—Yellow, three miles."

"Roger, Yellow, you are cleared for landing. Wind 010-10 knots."

The runway lay straight ahead of them. When they

came directly over the end, they would break off to the left in a sharp turn, fly along the runway downwind, and when they had come sufficiently far out, the planes would turn to the left toward the runway onto the base leg. Next the plane would turn into the runway and the last approach called the finale. During this time the planes would lose altitude, various checks would be made, wheels lowered, flaps and other things attended to.

Tore dreaded the landing itself somewhat. The K was considerably heavier and more difficult to handle at low speeds than the F-86-F. A plane ought to be set carefully on the ground, not dropped from the third floor with a clunk. There was always the danger that something would go wrong—a puncture, for example, or the possibility that the nose wheel would not tolerate the impact and break.

Knutsen came to the threshhold of the runway and broke off. Tore counted to five and broke off, too. In this way there would be adequate distance between the two planes. It was easy to take off in tight formation, but landing closely was not recommended.

Speed brakes out and a gradual descent. Tore checked the instruments for speed and pressure. He kept his hand at the throttle in case he suddenly found it necessary to gun the engine if he flew too low.

He swung into the base leg, put his hand on the landing gear handle, and lowered the landing gear. A slight shaking of the plane told him that the wheel well doors had opened and that the wheels were about to descend. A more powerful jerk in the fusilage indicated that the wheels were down and locked. The instrument in front of him showed a green light and three miniature wheels. Everything in order. All he had to do now was concentrate on the landing itself.

Tore thought he had come in a little too high and adjusted the throttle. The runway was coming at him much too fast. He was over the landing lights! Still too high. He wondered if he should gun the engine and go around again, but it would be too humiliating. Slowly he pulled the throttle all the way back, but this resulted in the plane's dropping too rapidly and with too great a loss of life from the wings. First one wheel hit the ground, then the other, and the plane lurched over heavily onto the nose wheel.

Tore swore silently in anger. What a landing! The worst he had ever done. Knutsen, who had already taxied off the runway, watched the whole thing and shook his head. He had never seen a worse landing. But then, the K wasn't the easiest thing in the world to set down.

Knutsen stood outside the hangar and waited for Tore to cut the motor after taxiing in. Lie waved Tore in easily, and all went well, though he was a bit weak in the knees after the jolting, unsuccessful landing.

The engine was cut, and silence fell once again over the hangar area. Stiff and sore, Tore climbed out of the cockpit, hopped onto the wing, and from there to the ground. He shook his head as Knutsen approached.

"Lousy landing. You'd better give the wheels a good going-over, Lie," said Tore, turning to the mechanic.

"Yeah—didn't look so hot." Knutsen sounded gruff, but when he saw Tore's despondent face, he had to smile.

"The K can take a lot more than that. Next time it'll go much better—you'll see." Knutsen smiled and gave Tore a friendly slap on the shoulder.

With their parachutes over their arms, the two pilots headed for the lounge as they chatted.

Tore was fairly satisfied, and Knutsen had no criticism. Tore liked Knutsen better and better. Actually it was a pretty decent squadron he had joined. At least his first impression was favorable.

Chapter 2

Training, Training, Training

The weeks that followed were hectic ones for Tore. He made a flight every day and advanced slowly but surely through the prescribed program. Everything had to be learned from the beginning, and progress was gradual. If something was poorly done, it was tried again.

To a pilot, every flight, every hour in the air is different from all the others. Training is based on being able to master every conceivable situation that might occur during a flight, no matter how routine it looks on paper.

The five first flights Tore flew with Knutsen, and he enjoyed himself hugely every time they were up. Knutsen was great to work with—always quiet and matter-of-fact, even when Tore made one error after another because errors were unavoidable in the beginning. Like all the others, Tore had his own method of piloting a plane, and the habits and quirks acquired from other aircraft had to be adjusted to the craft he was flying now—the K.

Knutsen kept the major informed of the progress and mistakes made on each flight. When a new pilot joins a squadron, he is always minutely observed in the beginning. There are some men who simply do not belong in a jet fighter and ought to be transferred. The first fourteen days usually showed what a pilot could do and indicated whether or not he really belonged in a jet squadron.

Tore never heard the results of the flights, only about the errors to be corrected the next time. But he felt he was making progress. True, he still flew a bit clumsily, and his landings in particular were nothing to brag about. He often admired the way Knutsen made a "grease landing" and had asked him how he did it.

"You've got to come in low with plenty of power and fly it down. I think you're holding the aircraft too high, and your nose is too high. It's pretty easy after you have enough landing hours under your belt." Knutsen sounded convincing when he said it.

Tore had tried to follow the advice about coming in low. But each time it had gone the same way, with perhaps not quite as hard a landing as before. Generally he had had far too much speed, making it necessary for him to use the drag chute, and that wasn't good.

Later he flew with one of the other pilots. He was to have two flights with each of them in the beginning in order to become acquainted with them and they with him. There were no regular flying partners in the squadron; it just depended on who was available when an order came in for a mission. Therefore, it was important that all the pilots were familiar with the way the others worked in the air.

There is seldom any problem in flying in good weather when the ground is always visible. It is something else when you have to make cloud penetrations and be completely dependent on the pilot leading down through the thick "soup." The wingman has only to follow the leader's slightest movement, but that can be difficult at times when you can barely glimpse the plane at your side.

Tore had yet to fly the K in bad weather. The fourteen days he had been with the squadron had been fair, with sun and little wind. Knutsen, however, had simulated bad weather and flown by instruments; he had had surveillance approaches and radar ground-control approaches. But it wasn't the same. Tore could peep to the side and see where he was and observe the aircraft's position in relation to the horizon, as well.

At Rygge, Tore had flown a lot in the clouds, so this type of maneuver was not totally unfamiliar to him. But he had to learn to fly through cloud cover in a new type of aircraft. He was glad the weather had been so good since it made it possible to get through the program a lot faster. For the present, he was not permitted to fly in the clouds—he had to complete the program first.

Tore had begun to adopt little tricks used by the various pilots in certain situations. No one made a dive or rolled out of a ninety-degree turn in quite the same way.

The men were nice, but they all had a slightly superior attitude since they had a lot more hours behind them than Tore. It was typical of the group that when they did aerobatics, they would try to shake Tore off their tails in the process; but no matter how hard they tried, Tore hung on. He was like an irascible terrier—if he clamped his teeth into a certain distance behind the lead plane, he clung there.

He sensed that the pilots had talked among themselves about this. He had carefully sounded Arild out, but the latter only smiled and shrugged it off with a joke.

Tore generally hung around with Arild, and he had the feeling that a real friendship was forming between them. At least they had a mutually friendly, confiding relationship. Tore had still not flown with Arild and wondered what he was like in the air.

Tore had been assigned a room beside Arild in the barracks, and the two of them would sit for hours discussing flying. Occasionally one of the other pilots would drop in, and the discussion frequently waxed hot and heavy. There was a good team spirit among the pilots, a mutual solidarity that included the major. They were all proud of the squadron. The pilots made a squadron a good one or a poor one, but it depended greatly on the squadron chief. Major Halse had a fine reputation among the pilots, and Tore liked all he had seen of him.

In addition to flying during the day, Tore had to plow through several hundred pages of written material about this new aircraft. To get the feel of the plane in the air was one thing; it was something else to be able to evaluate a defect that might show up during a flight and correct it without calling for help. Tore's aircraft had functioned without any particular flaws up to the present, and he thought Lie must be right when he said that it was the finest one in the squadron.

The plane had quirks or peculiarities that occurred at intervals, but these could be dealt with by acting correctly at the time. The only real dangers were total engine failure in the air or at takeoff, fire in the engine, hydraulic defects, or flying low enough to hit something. Some of the more serious accidents had their origin in poor judgment on the part of the pilot, but most of them were due to defects in the aircraft.

By reading reports and procedures for every conceivable dangerous situation, one could at least prevent certain errors. And if a critical situation occurred, one had to remember what to do in such a case. There were some situations that could only be handled with good sense and objective calculations, when everything depended on the experience and coolness of the pilot. Never lose your head, never give up without trying something.

Tore read all the material he could find, and nearly every evening he and Arild had a specific situation to discuss. If they were not in agreement, they called in an older flier, and it usually wasn't long before the whole barracks was involved in the discussion.

Tore felt increasingly that he was becoming a part of the squadron. He had been accepted by the other fliers—he was still green, but learning more every day.

One morning when the pilots had gathered for the briefing preceding the day's flights, the major came over to Tore, who was talking to Arild.

"How would you like to fly by yourself today, Bö?"

Tore was somewhat surprised by the question since it wasn't usual that one flew without a wingman at such an early stage.

"Yes, that would be great, Major, but I'm not sure if . . ." He left the decision to the major. He wondered eagerly what this meant.

"Well, you were to have flown with Nansen today, but he's flying a special mission, and none of the other men are free. I thought you might take a trip anyway in order to keep to the program."

The major had no doubts that Tore could fly alone, but the regulations stated that a new pilot should have a more experienced pilot on his wing for the duration of the training program.

Tore reflected. "There is something I'd like very much to do," he said. "I've had some problems with my landings. I wonder if I might fly an hour of landings so I can get the hang of it better."

The major looked surprised. He had expected something quite different. Any other new pilot would have welcomed an opportunity to fly on his own without someone's watching his slightest movement. Many would have used the chance for a few unlawful aerobatics, not to mention the temptation to fly low, very low.

"This boy's shaped in a different mold," thought the major. More ambitious, perhaps—more determined? Actually he had gotten that impression at their first meeting. It wasn't the first time the major had noticed that somewhat anxious, quiet boys could show real tenacity and toughness in order to stand out from among more self-assured fellows.

"Not a bad idea, Bö. It will be OK." He nodded briefly to the two men and proceeded to the duties awaiting him at the briefing.

Arild poked Tore in the side and whispered, "You've got the major's confidence. There aren't many who are permitted to fly alone this early in the game."

Tore listened carefully to the briefing even though it didn't affect him this time. Each pilot was given his assignment, and there was a slow and thorough examination of each flight. Tore was still not initiated into everything that went on in the squadron, but he under-stood that this was the beginning of something very important that concerned the entire squadron. He hadn't wanted to ask Arild, for he figured that if there were something he ought to know, he would find out about it in good time.

One by one the pilots left to ready themselves for the missions, and soon only Arild and Tore were left.

"We'll take a trip tomorrow. Work hard on your landings. Good luck!" Arild waved to Tore and swung his parachute over his shoulder. The silence in the room made Tore uneasy, but it was soon broken by the noise from the planes outside as the pilots started the engines. He had been directed to wait until everyone else was in the air. After that he could plan his own time.

Chapter 3

Forced Landing

"Tempo 33, Gardermoen. You are cleared for runway 02, wind is 350 degrees and 10 knots." It was the tower answering Tore's request for clearance to taxi out. Behind him roared the jet engine. All was ready.

Lie stood beside one of the wings and waved to him. Tore waved back. Lie had assured him the plane was in tiptop shape, and it handled that way.

Tore looked forward to the flight. He would be alone for a whole hour around the base, and he was determined to use the hour to good advantage. This time he would manage to make a decent landing with the K!

Tore responded to the tower's signal for clearance and gave the throttle the necessary forward tap to get the plane rolling. Soon he was safely settled at the end of the runway.

He went through the checklist much faster than he had done during the earlier flights, but the checks were carried out with the same precision as before. There was one situation in which a pilot had no right to hurry, and that was in carrying out the checks. You had to examine critically each figure and indicator. If there were something you didn't quite like, it mustn't be shrugged off as unimportant. The slightest irregularity demanded an immediate return to the hangar to get a possible defect corrected.

Tore had no reason to return this time; everything was functioning normally. He tightened his harness and adjusted his position in the seat. From habit he glanced out to the left to see if the wingman was ready, smiling when he saw he was alone—alone and absolute monarch. The strip was his, the plane was his, and the air around the base was his alone.

The brakes were released, and the pressure on his body in the seat increased as the plane gathered speed. The runway lights slipped by: first slowly, then more rapidly until they became a shining streak. He pulled gently on the stick, then a little harder, and the wheels left the ground. He was airborne.

He "cleaned" the plane of wheels and brake flaps and flew in a curve toward Lake Hurdal. He wanted to fly back and forth a bit before starting his landing rounds. It was like loosening up a little before climbing into a boxing ring and hitting hard.

"Gardermoen, Tempo 33 is clear to come in."

"Roger, you are alone. Call in at the finale."

Tore acknowledged this and made a wide, shallow turn toward the landing area. Prelanding checks went well, wheels were lowered, and he was clear for the approach.

For half an hour Tore kept on with his rounds. The first few landings were nothing to write home about. He tried various subtle adjustments and thought that the landings were gradually improving. After his tenth landing he needed a rest. The sweat poured off him inside his flight suit. He had concentrated so intensely that he found his entire body was stiff.

Tore radioed the tower and notified them that he was taking a trip northward and would return in five minutes. He was pleasantly satisfied; the last three landings had been tops.

He flew back and forth a little and let the plane glide forward in the air, up and down in small waves.

Five minutes passed all too quickly, and Tore prepared to come into the base again.

He received permission from the tower and began his prelanding checks again. His hand pulled the handle governing the landing gear, and Tore waited to feel the familiar jerk of the plane as the wheels lowered and locked. Nothing happened. He looked at the indicator. Hadn't he pulled the handle down far enough?

In front of him shone the three red lights indicating that the wheels were not down.

The thing he thought would never happen *had* happened. Suddenly he realized that it was happening to *him*. He must not lose his head. Carefully he drew the handle up again and shoved it down hard into position. Still nothing. He checked the hydraulic pressure, and it was in order. No problem there. Had he injured the landing gear during all those hard landings? It didn't help to think about that now. He looked for the fuel gauge and determined that he still had plenty of time at his disposal.

Thoughts flew through his mind. He saw before him the pages in the book describing just such a situation. For a moment he had two alternatives. One was to depress the emergency release for the wheels, and the other was to shake down the wheels with G force. He chose the former. Tore knocked away the safety cap on the emergency switch. The main switch was in the down position as it should be. With a flick of his finger he flipped the emergency switch and waited tensely for the result. Nothing.

He tried again, but with the same result. Negative.

So that wasn't working either. Tore was calm now that he knew what he had to do. When the malfunction first occurred, his heart had begun to pound and his hands shook. Now the first thing to do was to notify the tower.

"Gardermoen, Tempo 33 calling."

"What is it, Tempo 33?"

"I think there is something wrong with the wheels —can't get them out. Can you see if they have come out at all as I fly over the tower?"

A few seconds passed without anyone speaking. Tore was certain they had heard him, but it always takes a while before people are ready to tackle a really serious situation.

Now came the flight director's clear, calm voice through the ether to him. "OK. Come in. We'll take a look."

Tore knew that at the same moment the flight leader had pressed a red alarm button and that several squads at the base would be on emergency standby.

Tore swung around the tower and flew toward it. It had become unpleasantly warm in the cockpit, or else he was sweating profusely from nervousness. Over the tower he made a turn back and waited tensely for the reply.

"No wheels out, Tempo 33. Have you tried the emergency release?"

"Yes, it's not working. I'll try to shake them out now."

Tore drew the plane up to a higher altitude, not wanting to be too low when he had his mind on something besides flying. He was proud of the calmness of his voice over the radio, but inside he was anything but calm.

Tore flattened out at 5,000 feet and put the plane through short dives with rapid pullouts, attempting to shake out the wheels, but nothing happened. He worked for five minutes without a break, the sweat pouring off him, but to no avail.

"They don't move."

"Tempo 33, I have ordered the runway foamed down if you want to attempt landing without wheels."

Tore gave a start. He hadn't thought that far yet. He had been too busy with emergency procedures to think that perhaps he might have to make a belly landing.

The radio was silent.

"Tempo 33, do you read me?"

"Yes, I got it, but . . ." Tore cut off the words he had been about to utter.

"It will take fifteen minutes. How much fuel have you?"

Tore looked at the fuel tank and calculated quickly in his head. "About twenty-five minutes," he replied.

"OK. Fire engines are out there."

Now another voice came over the radio.

"Tempo 33 from Yellow leader, do you read me?" Tore recognized the quiet voice of the major, who was also in the air.

"Yes, Major."

"I understand you're in trouble. You can choose between two things, you know—either bail out or try to set the plane down on the foam strip being laid on the runway."

Tore had arrived at the same conclusion himself. He didn't really want to do either of the two, but he had to choose. He knew the risk involved in setting down a jet on its belly. The foam would work just like soap; the plane would slide over the runway instead of being torn by the hard cement. But what if he missed the strip? If he remembered correctly, it wouldn't be very wide.

But the decision was his. If he bailed out, he would most likely come down without a scratch, but the plane would be lost. In spite of everything, he felt a certain responsibility for that metal bird worth a couple of million. In addition, there was another factor strongly influencing him—the pride of a pilot. There had been plenty of belly landings that had been successful. Why shouldn't his be? Then he remembered that he didn't have many flying hours on his log; certainly very few compared to the experience of those who had accomplished such feats before.

Tore had decided.

"Major, I'm taking it in." There was a barely detectable quiver in his voice.

"OK, Tempo 33. I am directly over Eidsvoll now. Climb to 10,000 feet—you'll save fuel that way. Then circle over the base until the tower gives the go-ahead."

"Roger." Tore wanted to say as little as possible over the radio now, for he couldn't depend on his voice.

At the base there was tremendous activity. Two fire engines drove one behind the other, spraying a thin strip of foam from nozzled cannons mounted on their roofs. The plane would stop on a very small portion of the runway's total length, so it was not necessary to spray the entire runway.

Tore climbed in wide turns while he looked down at the white strip that grew longer and longer. How little it was! Could he manage to hit it? He was glad he had had that hour of landing practice. But this had to be done extremely delicately. Calculations, altitude, speed—everything had to work together perfectly. A chill swept down his back as he thought of how it could end.

Now he saw two planes approaching from the north. Must be the major and Knutsen, who were flying together today. The K climbed higher and soon had reached the indicated altitude.

"Tower, Tempo 33 is at 10,000 feet now. Circling left."

"OK. It ought not to be long now. We'll give a couple of minutes' advance warning so you can prepare for landing."

"Thanks," replied Tore.

"Tempo 33, we're coming up beside you. Just for company."

"Thanks, Major, I guess I could use a little. Care to exchange aircraft?" It helped to try a little joke.

The major laughed. Good thing the boy had his nerves under control. Now everything depended on Bö's ability to set the aircraft down according to the book. The major was painfully aware that it was no everyday affair for which the sergeant was preparing.

Suddenly Tore no longer felt so completely alone. Only a short time ago it had been wonderful to rule the air over the base, but now he was mighty glad of company. It gave him more self-confidence, and at the moment he needed all he could get.

Tore could imagine Lie standing by the hangar tearing his hair. His precious plane that never had gone on strike before!

Tore saw cars and trucks driving back and forth on the strip; there was frantic activity. Three ambulances were stationed at intervals along the runway. Would he need their services?

There was complete radio silence. Tore was glad, as he had no wish to engage in conversation with anyone at the moment. He reviewed what he would have to do. His plan must be completely clear as soon as he began to descend.

"Tempo 33, tower. When the last fire engine drives off the runway, we're clear. Good luck!"

Tore felt a knot in his stomach. Now there was no turning back. Yes, he could still jump, of course. But suppose he broke his leg in landing. And wouldn't the men in the squadron think he was a coward if he jumped now? He looked across at his two escorts. They smiled and signaled thumbs-up. Tore nodded, drew back on the throttle, and the plane went into a slow dive.

The two other planes withdrew to the side. They didn't want to hinder his movements, and he needed plenty of room. They lay behind him and followed him down. Tore had figured on coming in on a final long pass. It was important to aim the plane at the strip while he was still a good way off in order to avoid major corrections and to be able to concentrate on maintaining the proper altitude and speed.

The approach and the landing itself could not be the usual landing. He would have to fly the plane in on the strip and avoid any kind of rapid descent in the final phase. If he came in too high and the plane lost its lift, he would crash into the ground from a considerable height, and without the wheels to absorb the shock he would crack the plane in two. . . . He left the image incomplete.

He *had* to avoid a hard landing.

Altitude was down to 3,000 feet now, and he had swung far away from the area. He wanted that altitude at the beginning and then slowly to reduce it by an even and gradual descent.

He had told no one what he planned to do. The major watched the preparations eagerly and approved up to this point. He nodded to Knutsen, who was just as nervous on Tore's behalf as Tore himself. Knutsen admired Tore for what he was about to do. Would he have made the same decision if he had been in Tore's place? He thought so, but he had a lot more flying hours behind him.

In the tower there was dead silence; no one dared say anything. Tore must not be disturbed. What had to be said had been said, and all possible preparations had been made on the ground. Now it was up to the pilot to do the rest. The flight leader followed the plane with binoculars and saw that it was on a correct path toward the area.

Tore grasped the stick more firmly, sighted along the nose of the plane to get the desired angle, and pulled the throttle carefully back. He wanted to establish a descent of 200 feet per minute. That would give him a good overall view and an easy descent. He wiped the sweat from his eyes, feeling how wet he was inside his flight suit.

Now he must think of nothing except what he was about to do. It was easy to be distracted, and he had no time to waste.

Tore thought he was descending too slowly, and a glance at the altimeter told him he had lost only 500 feet. At this rate he'd miss the airport. He reduced the power even more and let the plane drop at a rate of 500 feet per minute . . . that was better.

Rapidly he went over what he must do just before he set the plane down. Cut all switches, stop the engine. He could cut the radio a little in advance as there was no need for it. He tightened his safety straps another notch; it was advisable to be securely harnessed since he could figure on rolling over if he were unlucky.

"Tower from Tempo 33. I'm cutting radio contact now."

"OK. Good luck!

"Yes, good luck, Tore." It was the major and Knutsen who took this final chance to give him self-confidence.

"Thanks, and out."

Tore switched off the radio and freed the wires. Now there was total silence around him. His feet, resting on the rudder pedals, began to shake, and he had to press them down firmly to quiet them.

He had reached 1,500 feet and the angle of glide looked fine, so he maintained the same drop. The white foam strip looked awfully narrow. It lay directly in front of the plane's nose and almost waved at him. "Try and catch me!" it said.

What would his mother and father think at this moment? Would they have preferred him to bail out? He saw his mother crying on his shoulder when he had informed them he would begin pilot training. No, he musn't think that way.

One thousand feet, the speed was good, nose perhaps a little crooked. He made a slight correction. There, now it was right!

In two minutes he would be down. He damned the wheels that wouldn't come down now that he needed them.

Three hundred feet, just right. Tore gave it more gas to reduce the drop; he still had two miles to go. Quickly he grasped the ejection mechanism for the canopy. He wanted to get rid of it so he could get out fast after landing. The canopy could jam during landing. He bent his head and pulled the handle. He heard a slight bang, and suddenly fresh air rushed into his face. It felt marvelous, even though the wind pressure was strong and unpleasant. The visor deflected it, however, so he could see clearly all the time. One mile left. More power—altitude was now only 200 feet.

The critical point was approaching. He watched the speedometer with an eagle eye. If he permitted the speed to drop too low, the plane would rear and crash into the ground. From a height of 200 feet it wouldn't be much fun.

The landing strip came toward him far too fast, but if he held the plane steady now, he would hit the middle of the foam. The speed and altitude had better be right! The altimeter indicated 100 feet. Now he was over the outer runway lights—yes, it was just right! The plane lay at only a slight angle and was losing only a few feet per yard.

Tore stared at the strip of foam as if hypnotized. He had to fly the rest by feel. His left hand rested on the throttle, and his right gripped the stick. Was he too high, perhaps? He was tempted to pull the throttle all the way back, but resisted. The altitude decreased ominously, and the plane began to be a little heavy to hold. Was he on the verge of stalling? Now there weren't many feet left to the ground. The plane had reached the edge of the foam strip just a few feet above ground.

Every eyewitness held his breath. "Now!" He was not aware that he had shouted the word. The throttle was pulled back to the "stop" position. The aircraft lost speed and all lift, falling like a boulder. Tore heard a soft scraping under the belly of the plane. Quickly he released the stick and cut every switch he could see.

Then he blacked out. The last thing he felt was his head being slung to the side and the terrific pain.

Now everything happened at once. The base's well-drilled emergency procedure took over. Two fire engines had driven down the strip after the aircraft, and it had barely come to a stop when it was doused in foam by both engines to extinguish all possible beginnings of a fire. At the same time, two firemen leaped from the running board and dashed to the plane, which had come to rest crosswise on the runway, one wing tipped sideways onto the cement.

Tore hung unconscious in the harness, but the two firemen freed him in seconds. Carefully they drew him out and supported him between them. An ambulance stopped beside the plane, and a stretcher was quickly hauled out. Tore was placed gently on the stretcher. The doctor bent over him and made a rapid examination. He straightened up and smiled reassuringly. The stretcher was lifted into the ambulance, which headed for the hospital with sirens screaming.

The major and Knutsen were cleared in on the cross strip, and they landed just as the ambulance disappeared. They knew nothing of Tore's condition, but they had seen the fine maneuvering along the final yards before the aircraft landed. Between the plane and the ground there had been a clearance of only a few feet when Tore had cut the engine. And the plane had set down nicely and continued straight along the foam strip. Just before the plane came to a stop it had swerved, for some reason, and ended up crosswise.

That was probably what had made Tore's head strike the corner of the cockpit with such an impact that he lost consciousness.

In the parking area, just before the major cut the engine, the tower called him.

"I can report that Sergeant Bö is fine. He got a cut on the head and a slight concussion." The flight leader's voice sounded relieved.

"Thanks very much." The major also was greatly relieved, and he smiled at Lie, who came running toward him. Tore's mechanic was almost green in the face, and he expected a harsh dressing down.

"Take it easy, Lie. Tore's fine, and the plane looks as if it had stood up pretty well."

"The pl-plane w-w-was in perfect shape before takeoff," stammered Lie. He felt partly to blame for what had happened.

"No one's blaming you, Lie," answered the major. "Things like that can happen to anyone in any aircraft."

The major slung his chute over his shoulder and walked toward the lounge, where he knew a lively discussion would be going on.

Chapter 4

Navigational Flying

The first thing Tore saw when he regained consciousness was Arild sitting on a chair beside the bed, reading a magazine. A low groan from Tore caused him to look up, and a broad smile spread across his face.

"Well, so you're in the land of the living again."

Tore wasn't sure at first why he was in bed, but gradually things came back to him.

"What happened?"

"According to the complimentary statements of all eyewitnesses, nothing," joked Arild. "The plane set down perfectly and slid along as if it had newly greased wheels. But just before it stopped, it got other ideas and swerved, tipping over on one wing."

Tore touched his head and felt that it was covered with a bandage. "So that's why I feel as if I'd been hit over the head with a sledge hammer!" Tore tried to smile and raise himself slightly, but he fell back with a groan. His head throbbed.

He wanted to ask Arild more questions, but Arild rose.

"I'll call the doc. He'll give you something to help you sleep so you can get in shape again." He went into the corridor and called Dr. Wide.

Tore hated injections, and he grimaced as Dr. Wide entered holding a syringe in his hand.

Arild chuckled sympathetically. He didn't much care for those sharp needles either.

"You can take a prick in the arm, can't you, Tore? You who doesn't let a sick K get you down?"

"OK, Doc, fire away." Tore shut his eyes and clenched his teeth.

"I've got to go. See you tomorrow, Tore," said Arild. "And sleep well. We've got a lot of catching up to do. Our flight tomorrow has been scrubbed."

"Thanks for coming, Arild." Tore's eyelids were growing heavy, and it wasn't long before he was in a deep sleep.

During the week that followed, the squadron pilots made it a habit to drop into the hospital every day, something Tore greatly appreciated. Time lay heavy on his hands, and he longed to fly again.

No one would say how long he had to stay there, but Knutsen had told him that he ought to figure on at least a week in bed. Fortunately, he had no other injuries except the mild concussion and the cut on his head.

Arild told him there was a lot of activity in the squadron at present because they were preparing for the annual competition for the navigation trophy, coveted by every squadron.

Each squadron was permitted a four-man team plus one reserve. Tore itched to get going again, but he was afraid he'd be too late. One week away from flying could mean a lot—and what if he were afraid to go up again?

He had been allowed out of bed the last couple of days, and he felt in good condition. Dr. Wide had promised to examine him thoroughly today. Tore wandered restlessly around the room and envied the others. He could watch the planes taking off just beyond the hospital. He knew Arild was sitting in one of them because his friend had just dropped in before going up to see how Tore was feeling.

There was a knock on the door, and Dr. Wide came in.

"Well, let's take a look at the patient." He rubbed his hands in high good humor. Tore sat on the edge of the bed, and the doctor began his examination. He even pressed hard on the side of Tore's head, but Tore remained expressionless despite the stab of pain it caused him.

"Mmmm—looking pretty good. I guess we'll cross you off the sick list tomorrow." The doctor looked questioningly at Tore, who was beaming.

"May I fly right away?" Tore waited anxiously for the answer.

"I'll call the major and recommend it. The sooner the better. But if you feel the least bit ill, you must come to see me."

"Sure—thanks, Doc—you're OK!" Tore shook him gratefully by the hand.

That night Tore dreamt about nothing but planes —two, four, many planes—a whole flotilla of jet planes.

The following day, when Tore joined the squadron, he was greeted by loud shouts of welcome.

Arild shook his hand warmly.

"Now we can really get going. The major has given me a free hand in getting you back in flying form again before a team is selected for the navigation competition."

Tore felt at home at once. Immediately afterward the two friends were eagerly planning the first flight, picking up right where they had left off. No one had asked Tore if he were afraid to go up again; it never even occurred to them.

Lie welcomed Tore back and showed him over to his new aircraft. X-ray was at the shop for overhauling.

58

The mechanic hovered around Tore while he made the exterior preflight check and assured Tore that he had gone over the plane with a magnifying glass and that everything ought to be in perfect order.

"I certainly don't blame you for what happened, Lie," said Tore. "It's seldom such a defect occurs, and it can happen to the best. You know that as well as I do." Tore punched Lie comfortingly on the shoulder as he climbed into the cockpit.

The checks went rapidly, for Tore hadn't been a lazybones while in the hospital. He had drilled himself over and over on the checklists and had read all the material the boys had brought along to him about flying, navigation, and blind flying.

Tore closed the canopy and looked over at Arild, who gave him the thumbs-up signal.

Did he feel anxious as he sat there waiting to take off again? Tore hadn't had time to reflect on it. His hands and his thoughts had been occupied with what they had been trained to do, but now as he sat at the end of the runway and waited for the departure signal, he felt a slight sinking in his stomach. What if . . . ?

Tore shook his head and let his thoughts circle around other things. Intently he watched a plane coming in for a landing, and by the style he knew it was Knutsen.

"Yellow 1 and 2, you are clear now." It was the signal from the tower.

Tore gave it the gas and swung out on the runway, closely followed by Arild.

The familiar thrill swept through him again when he kicked the afterburner in and felt the plane struggling to get loose, as if it yearned to do its best to satisfy him.

Before he knew it, he was airborne, and a glance to the side told him that Arild was on his wing.

First they were to fly around a little so that Tore could become familiar with this new aircraft. Then they were to take off on their first navigational trip. They had chosen four checkpoints, which were first to be located and then flown over at a given time.

In in-flight navigation it is not simply a matter of finding one's way as in an orientation race on the ground. In the air it is necessary to fly over the checkpoints within a time interval of plus or minus ten seconds. It was this they were to train for on the first flights: precision and greater precision.

Tore would do all the flying himself the first day, and Arild would observe and note his errors.

"Yellow 1 from Yellow 2. Time minus 5." That was Arild informing Tore that he had five minutes left before starting on the first leg—the term they used to designate the first run from point A to B.

"Roger, Yellow 2."

Tore turned toward Eidsvoll. Just over the railway station the first leg would begin. Tore glanced at his knee where the map was fastened by a clip. He adjusted the throttle to the desired speed and climbed 500 feet to have the correct altitude.

Eidsvoll lay directly beneath him, and he still had

three minutes left. He broke off to the left and chose to twist the plane at an angle that would give him a 360-degree turn in slightly under three minutes. Arild followed him all the time. No extraneous words were exchanged on the radio.

Tore could hear the other pilots in the squadron check in on the tower frequency as they came in for landing. It was fun to feel the activity around him again and know that he was a small part of the whole.

The turn was completed. A quick glance at the clock showed that he was ten seconds too early. No help for it, he'd have to try to drop those seconds on the next leg.

Tore swung the plane into the course he had calculated on the ground. It was not until you got into the air that you could tell if all the calculations made before starting were correct. A weather report for the route was obtained from the meteorologist, and the pilot made his own calculations on the computer to determine the proper altitude and speed. He had also to consider the head wind, wind drift, and variations between the ground and flying altitude. Temperature in the air is important as well, since it influences engine performance and fuel consumption. The computer then shows which speed, altitude, and course a plane must hold in order to cover a given distance in a given time. The pilot himself decides the engine power necessary to hold the calculated speed.

In the air, there were an unbelievable number of things that had to be done almost simultaneously. The instruments must be constantly checked. Landmarks passing beneath the plane must be compared with the map so the pilot always knew his location and could determine if the course was correct. It was necessary to keep an eye open in all directions, too—you weren't alone in the air, even if it might seem that way.

Tore and Arild were now approaching checkpoint B, which was a small lake, or at least they ought to be according to the clock, but no matter in which direction Tore searched, he couldn't see it. He had only forty-five seconds left. Had he flown the wrong course? No, the log map said 104 degrees, and he was holding 104 degrees. There ought to be a slight elevation just before the lake; perhaps that was why he couldn't see the surface of the water. If only the time was right. Yes, there ahead was the slight ground elevation. Two degrees to the left, 102 degrees by the compass. Twenty seconds left. He'd be too late. Tore resisted the temptation to give it a little extra gas. This wasn't permitted in the competition since it would immediately affect the fuel consumption, which would be carefully checked. Tore swept over the high ground, and the water lay directly beneath him. He noted down the time to the second and turned quickly into the new course.

"Minus 20, Yellow 1," came teasingly from Arild. Nothing more.

The rest of the flight went in a similar fashion. Tore was always either too early or too late over the various checkpoints, and he perspired more than was good for him. He was completely soaked under his flight suit, his limbs felt heavy as lead, and he would have given anything for a glass of cold beer.

The landing went mechanically, and, remarkably enough, it was a good landing. Tore was exhausted. His concentration during the flight had been intense. He had probably been far too tense and eager to carry out his assignment without a single error. He was glad when he felt the wheels roll down the landing strip and he could finally relax. But he couldn't relax completely until he sank exhausted in the deep armchair in the briefing room.

Arild was very nice about it. He had a lot to point out, but he did it in a calm and friendly way. Tore shook his head.

"I just wasn't with it today. I had the feeling that the plane was flying me instead of the other way round," he said.

"No, you weren't in top form, but don't worry about it. You can't have a week's vacation without pay-ing for it, but you'll soon have your hand in again." Tore smiled weakly and nodded, but he had little con-fidence in the comforting words. He would never learn to do a good job of navigational flying.

"How's for a game of billiards at the mess hall to get our minds off things?" Arild rose and sauntered out to the jeep. And it wasn't long before the two friends were trying to get the better of one another at the bil-liard table.

After each flight Tore felt he was making some progress, but he also felt it was going far too slowly. There was only one week before the squadron team was to be chosen. He had made five trips with Arild now, and they flew well together—Arild was extremely pleased with his progress. He had mentioned this to the squadron chief one day when he was called into the office to make a report on Tore after the accident.

"Things seem to be going in the right direction for him. Teach him everything you can in the short time remaining, Nansen," said Major Halse. "We'll see what happens. I have a hunch he's going to be really good—he's got guts, that boy, but he's got a lot to learn yet. Good luck, Lieutenant!"

Arild was in a good mood when he left the office, and Tore was about to ask him why he looked so happy. He was sitting in full flying equipment, waiting for Arild. They were to take their sixth and final flight before Saturday, since all the pilots were to have a day off before the final selection was made.

Tore and Arild had decided to take a trip to Oslo, and they were to leave as soon as their last flight was over.

Lieutenant Knutsen watched them as they planned the trip. They had become close friends, he had noticed. In the air he could see the kind of precision they had when they flew together. It was as if each one knew what the other was thinking and would do. He had also observed them closely one day when they had fooled around a bit with hair-raising aerobatic maneuvers. Occasionally the two planes had looked as if they were glued together, not dangerously close, but in precisely the correct position for such maneuvers. The two pilots had not noticed him flying like a hawk high above them, nor had he said anything over the radio that would give them any indication that he was there.

Major Halse had given Knutsen the job of observing and noting down anything that might be of interest. This report had been passed on to the major and was full of pluses. The major had been extremely pleased.

Knutsen watched the two of them disappear, and shortly afterward he heard the whine from the jet engines that told him they were taxiing out.

Knutsen was no newcomer to the tension that selection for the navigation competition carried with it. He had been a member of the squadron team for three years, but Squadron 666 had never placed better than third in the championship. Even if one of the four flew exceptionally well, or even two of them, it was their teamwork that counted. He wondered who would participate this year. He was betting on Arild as one of the most likely. As for the major, there was no question. He had always been the best of them all.

If he included himself, there was only one remaining place on the team. Arild had told him one evening about Tore's ability to find his way to unknown areas in the wink of an eye, though Tore himself was not aware of how good he was. Yes, Knutsen thought, Tore had an excellent chance of being the fourth man on the team if he flew equally well during the selection flights.

Well, Saturday would tell the tale.

Tore and Arild had greatly enjoyed their trip to Oslo. Generally when two pilots are together, there is a lot of talk about flying, but the two of them had talked mostly about other things—about their families and private affairs—and had become better acquainted than ever.

Saturday morning the entire squadron was gathered once again in the squadron building. The big day had finally arrived.

The run to be flown had been drawn up by two pilots in Squadron 667, who were also to serve as judges.

From this point on, it was each man for himself; each would show what he had learned during all the previous flights and hours of training.

Tore prepared as he always did when under pressure. He had drawn number one and was to fly first. This was an advantage because it meant he would avoid even more nervous build-up and tension before his turn to fly.

At the very moment the clock on the wall struck nine, his name was called. He walked forward and received his envelope, opened it on the way to the plotting table, and had everything ready. Five minutes later he was on his way out to the plane with an eager expression on his face. As he passed, he flashed a smile to Arild and Knutsen, who were waiting their turns.

Lie was on the spot, and the checks went as smoothly as butter—nothing was omitted. Everything happened so quickly that Tore was in the air almost before he knew it and on course toward the first turning point. He checked the time, altitude, and speed and settled down in his seat. His nervousness was gone, and he was calm and calculating.

At the first point he erred by five seconds, which wasn't too bad. A few errors popped up underway, but he discovered them quickly and reported rapidly and precisely over the radio what he saw. No unnecessary jabber; that counted as a minus.

When he came in to Gardermoen for landing, he couldn't believe he had completed the whole thing; it struck him as almost miraculous.

The landing was beautiful, and he taxied in to Lie, who waved him into place, eager to hear how things had gone. But it was impossible to know how Tore had placed. Not until the last pilot had landed would the calculations and discussions between the judges take place and the final results be posted.

Tore removed his flying gear and walked over to the mess hall to rest. The participants were not permitted to talk to anyone before the last man had landed.

No one was in the mess hall, and Tore settled down in a corner to read a magazine.

Someone was shaking his arm. Tore opened his eyes; he must have fallen asleep sitting there. He looked up into Arild's smiling face, and directly behind him stood Knutsen.

"You were number two, right behind the major!" burst out Arild joyfully, and whacked him on the shoulder.

Tore blinked a few times before he realized what they were saying. He rose, still confused. "Me . . . ? Next best?" He had realized he was pretty good now, but that surpassed his highest hopes.

Knutsen cleared his throat and reported that the squadron team would consist of the major, naturally, Arild, himself, and Tore—exactly as he had predicted.

Now the tough training would start. All four would fly together as a team, taking turns leading, planning, and giving orders. Tore looked forward to it. He finally had proof that he'd made it as a pilot, even though he still had plenty to learn.

Chapter 5

Norwegian National Championship

The national championship was scheduled for the following Sunday at Gardermoen, and the entire week was devoted to intense training. Formation flying was given first priority. The major led the flights in the beginning since he had had the most experience, but the pilots learned quickly, and Tore went in for the training body and soul. To be one of "the big ones" was quite an experience for him, and he stored up each piece of information for later use.

When they had become more proficient in formation flying, they took turns being in the lead in every type of unusual situation. The major kept close tabs on the errors made by each pilot and corrected them conscientiously afterward. He was more than satisfied and told the men that rarely had he seen a team as closely welded together. Praise never hurt anyone.

After Friday's flight they sat in the major's office and discussed the final details.

"All right, boys, this was our last trip until the competition on Sunday. I've decided to give you extended leave so you'll be in top form."

"Great!" shouted Arild, seeing Oslo beckoning in the distance.

"Yes, you've all earned a break. I'm extremely pleased with your efforts up to now. Keep it up and things will go great on Sunday. Be home Saturday evening and turn in early. That's all. Have a good trip." The major rose, and the others saluted and left the room.

"Why don't we take Dr. Wide's boat? He offered to lend it to me any time," Tore told Arild when later they were discussing what they might do on Saturday. Arild was quite willing to give up the trip to Oslo. Tore's plan sounded fine to him.

"Great idea. We can sign out a tent and fishing poles from the Recreation Division. What a trip we'll have!"

Dr. Wide said yes at once when Tore asked if they might borrow the boat and told him where it was anchored in Lake Hurdal. Tore promised him part of the catch in exchange. The doctor merely smiled, for there weren't many fish at this time of year.

Tore and Arild got everything ready. They had been able to borrow a jeep from the major, and into it went fishing rods, food, and coffeepot. Arild drove in his customary fashion, at top speed and with screaming tires.

When Dr. Wide was finally finished with his Saturday appointments, he sat in his office working at a sheaf of reports.

"Come in," he said with irritation upon hearing a knock at the door. He didn't even glance up to see who it might be. A peculiar odor made him swing about in his chair, and he found himself staring into the black glassy eyes of two enormous fish. Behind the fish stood two grinning young men whose words of, "Help yourself!" tumbled over each other.

"Well, if this isn't a pleasant surprise! Did you buy them to fool me?" the doctor said with a laugh.

Both boys were eager to tell the tale, and the doctor heard the fish story from beginning to end.

"Well, I surely do thank you. If you'd like to borrow the boat again, just let me know. This was a delightful interruption on a tiring Saturday afternoon. Not to mention the prospect of having fresh fish for supper!"

Tore and Arild reported to the major and thanked him for the jeep. It was their idea to eat supper and go to bed.

"How would you like to have supper at my place tonight?"

Arild and Tore looked at each other and then thanked the major eagerly. It was a delightful evening. The major's wife served a delicious meal, and after supper they sat in front of the fire and listened to Mrs. Halse play the piano. For a few hours, at least, they were not thinking about flying.

At ten o'clock they said their good-byes, full of good food and in excellent spirits.

"Shake a leg, Tore! It's eight o'clock!" Arild, fully dressed, was shaking Tore.

"Wha' . . . eight? But . . ."

Arild laughed. If it had really been eight o'clock, they should have been gathered in the briefing room in the squadron hall.

Tore staggered out of bed, reeled over to the sink, and stuck his head under the cold running water. He was still only half awake. He glanced at his watch and was relieved to see that it was only a little after seven.

Arild looked fresh and wide awake. Tore envied him. The very thought of the approaching competition tied his stomach in knots. Didn't *anything* bother Arild?

"Get a move on so we can grab a bite of breakfast before they close up shop. I'd like a nice walk in the sunshine."

Tore looked out of the window and saw the sun rising over the hilltops under a cloudless sky—perfect flying weather. The pale stubble of his beard disappeared during a quick once-over with the electric shaver, and he dressed rapidly.

"How are you feeling?" asked Arild on the way out.

"Ghastly. My stomach's doing flip-flops and my mouth's completely dry." Tore attempted a smile, but it turned into a grimace.

"Me, too," answered Arild.

There were already several men gathered at the breakfast table, and Tore greeted some old friends from Rygge and flight school. The chatter was lively, and chances of winning the championship were eagerly debated. Stories were exchanged, and the mood was exhilarating.

After eating Tore and Arild quietly withdrew and walked slowly over to the squadron building. All the aircraft stood polished and newly trimmed, lined up like tin soldiers. The mechanics were busy with the final checks. They took everything even more seriously than usual today.

The four planes to be used in the competition stood at the far side of the taxi strip, and Tore saw Lie bent over the cockpit of one of them.

"Hi, Lie, something the matter?" Tore called.

Lie looked up and shook his head. "Nope, just an extra check on the oxygen system."

"Glad you're so thorough. We don't want to make many mistakes today."

"You're right! The boys have gone over the planes

with a magnifying glass, and they've never been in better shape."

Tore knew that when Lie said so, it was so. He wasn't one to avoid any kind of work. Still, things could go wrong that no one could prevent in advance.

"Take it easy," said Tore, and raised two crossed fingers.

It was close to eight o'clock, so Tore and Arild walked to the squadron building, which was to be the gathering place. There they found a spot beside Knutsen, who was deeply engaged in conversation with a pilot from Bodö.

"Hi, men, how's your form?" Knutsen smiled encouragingly. Tore nodded and sat down without answering. He couldn't very well say he was nervous and had butterflies in his stomach.

"Attention!" The command was heard in the background. Everyone rose and stood stiffly at attention.

General Nilsen and his adjutant came down the center aisle, followed by the base commander. When the general had stepped up on the platform, he turned to the men and said, "Good morning, men."

"Good morning, General," came the reply in unison.

The general began to explain the rules and scope of the competition. "Five minutes before each pilot's start he will receive an envelope. The contents will tell him what to do. How well he does depends on his previous training. The standard in the Air Force has always been high, and previous results have been of the best.

We hope the same will hold true today—and that the best pilot and the best squadron will win." The general sat down, and the base commander, Colonel Dahle, took the platform.

"During this championship competition," he began, "you will encounter various difficult tests. I can only say that you'd better have your eyes and ears open. And now I'll give you your starting numbers."

The pilots sat tensely and waited. Tore gripped the pencil he had brought for making notes. Pretty soon everything would break loose. Had he learned enough to pass the test well? Would he disappoint the others who were depending on him?

"Sergeant Tore Bö—number five," he heard the colonel say. Tore jumped. He would be the first of his own squadron's pilots to fly. He felt sorry for those who had to wait until the end. For them it would be a trial of nerves as well as skill.

Tore looked at his watch—0855 hours. Five minutes left before the first man would begin. He still had half an hour to sweat it out.

"Number ten," he heard Arild whisper. That meant he'd be about twenty-five minutes behind Tore.

"Well, that's all." The base commander gathered his papers together. "Good luck, and give it real effort!" The commander left the platform.

Everyone stood at attention until the general and his group had left the room. Then bedlam broke out among the pilots. They had to change to flying togs, and small prechecks were made. As the starting time approached for each pilot, he would go to the briefing room and begin planning and calculating. The time would be clocked from the moment the pilot entered the room.

Tore walked silently beside Arild and Knutsen. The major had disappeared during the din, probably into his office.

The three men dressed in silence and checked to see that their G suits fitted correctly and were tight enough. The oxygen masks were tested and the helmet straps fastened.

"That looks good," said Knutsen. "Let's go in to the major."

They walked toward the door which was suddenly opened by the major himself. "Come on in! I was just going out to look for you. Sit down."

They seated themselves around the desk.

"I don't have much to say to you. Just use your own judgment. I am positive everything will go well. If you stick to the same path you've been following, I have no worries. How are your nerves holding up, Bö?"

"I don't know, Major. Stomach ache and sweating," replied Tore.

"That's good," said the major. "Without those things you wouldn't be in shape. I feel limp myself. After all, who wouldn't be?"

The major smiled briefly and lit a cigarette. He looked at the time. "I won't keep you any longer. Bö, you have ten minutes left, and there are probably a few things you'd like to check before starting. Well, best of luck, boys!"

"Take it easy, Tore," said Arild when they were outside again. "Watch I don't catch up to you in the air!"

Tore was deep in his own thoughts. "Yeah, good luck to you, too." He walked toward the toilet.

Now he was alone . . . only five minutes left. He made a final check for pencils, writing pad, compass, and navigational computer. All in order.

One minute ahead of time he walked slowly over to the briefing room, where a table had been placed outside the door. Behind it sat one of the pilots who would not participate in the competition. He looked at the stopwatch on the table, reached out for an envelope on which was written the number five, and handed it to Tore. To his own amazement Tore found that his hand did not shake as he took the envelope.

"Good luck," he heard dimly as he opened the door and walked through.

On the way to the plotting table he opened the envelope and stared at the contents. There were six different groups of numbers, and he soon saw that they were numbers indicating a certain map and a certain place on the map. To make things difficult, they had been given only map references instead of names.

On the plotting table lay a pile of maps, and he quickly found the correct one, spread it out, and placed the coordinates on it. Soon the route began to take form. The first checkpoint was in the vicinity of Storsjöen, northeast of Gardermoen; then further northeast to Finnskogen near the Swedish border.

From there due west to Dokka, then southward to Norefjell, east again to Hönefoss, and back to Klöfta, where the final checkpoint was located.

The checkpoints did not lie directly in the middle of these spots, but slightly outside. On the slip of paper he had received, it said that the points would be marked by a large red and white flag. He'd better keep his eyes peeled when approaching these places.

When the route was finally mapped out, it was simple enough to determine the distance and to calculate speed and time, always taking into consideration the given altitude and flight level, which were also written on the paper.

Tore was extremely careful with his calculations. He knew that the basis for success was the work done on the ground. There wouldn't be time for any calculations after he was in the air, so it was essential to calculate as accurately as possible now, preferably to the second. When he had finished, he double-checked and was satisfied. He stared intently at the route he had laid out and noted certain important details of the terrain over which he was to fly. It would be an advantage to have the route in his head as far as possible so that he knew in advance what he should be watching for. Because of the speed of a jet, one must always have one's attention ahead of the plane itself or it might be too late.

Tore stuffed the log cards in his pocket, together with the map and other equipment he had used, and trotted out the door leading to the parking area.

Lie stood beside the plane and waved eagerly to Tore. He was holding the parachute ready and helped Tore on with it.

"Everything's all clear. I've gone over the plane myself with a fine-toothed comb, and there isn't a blemish on her," announced Lie proudly. Tore had complete confidence in the mechanic, but as a double-check he took a quick turn around the plane to see if there were any loose parts or small errors that Lie had overlooked anyway. Everything appeared in perfect order.

Lie leaned over Tore in the cockpit, tightened his harness, and removed the safety pins from the seat. Tore was busily checking all the instruments before takeoff.

Lie hopped down and signaled thumbs up. Tore engaged the starter and immediately heard the buzzing and rumbling that told him the engine had caught.

He signaled Lie to detach the starting wagon and adjusted his position to give him a better view of the instruments as they reacted to the engine. A buzzing in his ears told Tore that the radio had warmed up and was switched on. He didn't need to glance even once at the checklist, which he had placed on his knee for safety's sake. Now he knew every check by memory, backward and forward.

Tore checked in by radio. "Blue 5 ready to taxi."

"Roger, Blue 5. You are cleared for runway 02, the wind is 030 and 08 knots, altimeter 30.09."

Tore repeated the runway, wind, and altimeter

reading, which he then set so that it showed in the little window in the altimeter. Now the altimeter would indicate his exact height above sea level.

While this was going on, Tore had released the brakes and was on his way out to the runway. Lie waved to him and he waved back.

Not until now did he notice something hanging from the far-right corner of the instrument panel. He looked more closely and discovered that it was a little mascot, a troll with long black hair, riding on a broomstick. He recalled having seen it in Lie's room.

So Lie had given him his mascot—that was darned nice of him! He hoped it brought good luck.

Tore was very careful with the throttle since the fuel had been carefully measured when the tank had been filled. This made it possible to figure how much fuel he had used. This amount, in turn, would be compared to what he had calculated that he would need and written on his log card.

Just before he stopped, prior to rolling out on the runway, he heard the tower. "Blue 5, you are clear for entry and takeoff, wind 030 and 06 knots."

"Gardermoen, Blue 5 read. Thanks."

Tore headed the plane down the yellow midstrip and applied the brakes. Full throttle and the afterburner caught. Next, a rapid sweep of the eyes over all the instruments, which were within the range of the green arcs on the indicators. Then he released the brakes and felt how the plane picked up speed as it sped down the strip.

Ninety knots and he pulled gently on the stick. The

nose lifted from the ground. One hundred and ten knots and he felt the plane straining to leave the ground.

Suddenly he was in the air, climbing to 5,000 feet, which was the altitude for the first "leg."

Carefully he selected the angle of climb and the cruise power he had calculated on the ground. He had to depend on his calculations until he had passed the first checkpoint; then he could see if they were accurate. The meteorologists often estimate the wind incorrectly, in which case he would have to make the necessary corrections.

He held a steady course at 053 degrees and leveled off at an altitude of 5,000 feet. A check with the clock —exactly according to plan. Tore smiled and settled more comfortably into his seat. The plane performed smoothly. The speedometer was glued to the indicated speed he had correctly estimated, and he maintained his height within a few feet.

From now on his attention must be equally divided between the inside and outside of the plane. Contact with the terrain was extremely important, and he was aware that several tests of observational ability were included in the run.

As he passed the Vorma River, he noticed that there were several trucks lined up along one of the banks. Closer examination revealed that several tanks were placed between the vehicles. He counted six and hastily noted on the pad resting on his knee the place, time, and number of vehicles.

Over the radio he could hear the pilots reporting in

from their checkpoints—short, concise reports. There were four men ahead of him. Soon it would be his turn if he ever found the checkpoint over Storsjöen.

Storsjöen appeared ahead of him, even though there were still a few minutes left. He maintained a perfect course toward the southern end of the lake exactly where the checkpoint ought to be if his calculations were correct. He had to depend on them. He checked the time and found the calculations would work out quite well. Now it was a matter of keeping an eye out for the red and white flag. At the southern end of the lake there should be a little peninsula, and if he hadn't guessed wrong, the point would be placed there. He figured that the first checkpoint would be easy to find; it would give the pilots confidence and create a certain calm during the remainder of the flight.

Exactly as he had thought. In the middle of the peninsula waved a large flag, red with white stripes.

"Gardermoen. Blue 5 over checkpoint A—Alpha."

"Roger, Blue 5. Noted."

Tore checked the time, entered it in the log, and added on the time he had calculated it would take to the next point.

At the same time the plane turned to the left as the nose pointed upward. He would climb to 10,000 feet now. Tore reacted automatically. He and the plane were one. It obeyed his slightest command, filling him with pleasure. All the instruments were quiet, vibrating within the permissible limits. The fuel gauge showed how much he had left, and it agreed with his notations. He had been eight seconds too early. Perhaps this was due to more tailwind than he had figured on, but it was so slight that he decided not to alter speed, and he kept to the cruise power he had calculated.

Just before reaching 10,000 feet he gradually began to lower the nose in order to level off evenly at the correct altitude. The course remained at 046 degrees, and the speed increased to 305 knots, where it stabilized.

Storsjöen lay far behind him now. From this altitude he had a glorious view in all directions. Everything appeared in miniature, but extremely clearly. Roads, rivers, houses, and cars were easy to pick out. He speculated as to the nature of the observation test that might have been inserted at this point. Perhaps there was none, but he kept a sharp lookout.

Tore tried to visualize the terrain according to the map. He recalled that there was dense forest near checkpoint B—nuts, it would be a lot more difficult to find than the one by Storsjöen.

Over the radio he heard Blue 4 call from checkpoint B—Bravo, and Tore thought the pilot sounded slightly annoyed. He checked the time and found he had overtaken Blue 4 by two minutes. In other words, the latter must have had some trouble finding the place. Tore stroked the mascot, which hung and swung happily from the instrument panel. The troll had probably never been so high up before.

Tore made some slight calculations with reference

to the town of Elverum, which he could see far to his left. Things seemed to fit pretty well. The distance was still too great for him to be able to take accurate bearings. He would be crossing the Glomma River just southeast of Flisa in a few minutes. Here he could estimate the exact time. On the map he had placed five-minute interval markers, which he checked off as he flew over the points. The next marker was just beside the Glomma.

Tore glanced to the left and had Flisa at about ten o'clock. He saw the Glomma clearly, winding along like a snake.

But what was that? He checked with the map. Ought there to be a bridge here? He looked for the date on the map. It was quite new. So a new bridge had appeared since the map had been drawn. Or could it be a bridge that the Engineering Corps had constructed? It was difficult to see from such an altitude, but to be on the safe side, he noted it down with the accurate position. He flew over the Glomma, and the time agreed almost exactly. If only the rest went equally well! There was supposed to be a small lake near the checkpoint, which lay just southwest of Finnskog.

He couldn't see any water ahead yet—it was hidden by the dense woods. He might fly over the point without seeing it. If he messed this up, he would have to make a 360-degree turn and hunt around. He'd lose a lot of time that way. This was probably what had happened to Blue 4.

The time was dangerously close, and the nose of the plane would obstruct his vision straight downward. Tore had decided what he would do. He would count on having held the correct course and speed. When about five seconds remained, he would flip the plane onto its back.

Tore counted the seconds to himself. Ten, nine, eight, seven, six, five—the stick quickly to the right, and Tore lay with his head down and stared into the shining surface of a lake. And there, just to the right, was a clearing in the woods where blue smoke rose from a chimney. On the roof had been painted, or spread out, a large red and white flag. On the button again! He rejoiced as he straightened out the aircraft. The first thing to do was to send a message.

"Gardermoen, Blue 5 over checkpoint B—Bravo."

"Roger, Blue 5. Time noted." Tore knew that the same report was sent over the ground radio to the observer sitting in the cabin below drinking coffee. In this way the reports were subject to double control.

Tore had pulled the throttle almost all the way back, and he continued to glide in a turn to the left on a course of 280 degrees. He would descend to 3,000 feet on the next stretch. He was careful to keep the speed down. This he did with the aid of the speed brake and angle of the nose in relation to the ground. Ascents and descents had been minutely calculated beforehand. The way the calculations had worked so far, Tore was ready to depend on them blindly for the rest of the trip. The view from 3,000 feet would be poor;

one couldn't see as far ahead and must watch intently for each control point.

The air was far less stable down here, and Tore strapped himself tightly. The throttle was pushed slowly forward as he approached 3,500 feet, and the nose lifted gently. The plane assumed the correct position, and the number of revolutions were adjusted according to the log. He would fly directly over Hamar and Gjövik, and he had estimated the time he would pass over them.

Hamar was passed first with five seconds to spare, but Tore maintained the same speed. He had seen nothing unusual to note down, although it was better to note too much than too little. He kept a particularly close lookout for military movements or positions.

Gjövik, too, was passed with five-plus seconds, and Tore drew back on the throttle almost imperceptively, although he was conscious of the effect.

Dokka was only a few minutes away now, and Tore strained to catch sight of both the river and the railroad tracks. It was difficult to say if the checkpoint lay to the left or the right of the tracks, but it should be due south of the station building.

The plane had behaved perfectly the entire time. Tore had more than half the route behind him now, and everything had gone well—almost suspiciously well. Tore nodded to the troll, which nodded back in time with the swaying of the plane.

Suddenly the railroad tracks appeared slightly to his right. He was a bit off course; they should have been on the left of the plane. A quick check and a slight correction and he was in position again. He couldn't see any flag, or rather only the Norwegian flag that waved from its pole on a tiny house due south of Dokka. Or was it a Norwegian flag? He had assumed it was, since it was flown from a flagpole. No, by jiminy, it was red and white! Lucky again! If he hadn't taken a second look at the flag, he would have been fooled.

"Gardermoen, Blue 5 over checkpoint C—Charlie."

Gardermoen replied that they had received the message.

Once more a turn to the left, 212 degrees this time, and even lower down. This leg would be flown at 500 feet above the terrain the entire time, and this was tiring. One must be sure to maintain the same height over the ground all the time. This meant climbing and descending according to variations in the terrain. Nor were there any control points on the route until he crossed Kröderen, and that was just before the checkpoint itself. Here he must depend entirely on his previous calculations. This stretch covered mostly deserted woodland, which was probably the reason they were permitted to fly so low.

The landscape rushed beneath him, and Tore could see that he had flushed many birds. He refused to think what might happen if he collided with a bird at this speed. He had heard that it was like flying into a projectile.

On this stretch it was unlikely that any observation test had been included; there was barely time to notice

if one flew over a lake or a river. No, he'd fly blind by
the clock and "let the devil take the hindmost." He
would undoubtedly notice Norefjell, a well-known
mountain, for it lay one thousand feet higher up. The
leg he had planned would cut across the top to the
right, and the checkpoint ought to be there, too. But
what if it lay on the other side? Well, he'd just have to
circle like a top around the summit until he found it.

Where was the northern tip of Kröderen? Had he
passed it? No, otherwise he would have seen the Hal-
lingdal River, which emptied out here. He began to be
nervous, even though he still had thirty seconds before
he was charted to arrive.

Suddenly he saw something glittering ahead of the
plane. He cut over exactly at the mouth of the river. A
slight turn to the left, only two degrees, because he
should have been a little to the south. Now only one
minute remained until he was due to have reached the
summit of Norefjell. He'd really hit it this time, for he
could see the peak rising just to the right of the plane's
nose. The walls were very steep on this side, and Tore
wondered how it was possible to establish a checkpoint
there. He approached at considerable speed and decided to pull up to gain some height and thereby a better view.

At that moment, directly ahead, he saw a plateau
where a tent had been rigged. Or was it a parachute?
At any rate, it was red and white!

Tore could not contain himself. He pointed the
nose downward and dove straight to the spot. At fifty

feet he pulled straight up and made an elegant roll to indicate that he had made a hit. Simultaneously he pressed the sender.

"Gardermoen, Blue 5, checkpoint D—Delta."

"Roger, Blue 5. But cut the aerobatics."

Tore was embarrassed. He had forgotten that the observer was in direct radio contact with the tower and had been able to report the unlawful diving attack.

A sharp turn to the left again and the plane set a course for Hönefoss at 071 degrees. Tore climbed to 5,000 feet again. It was more pleasant and relaxing at that altitude.

On this leg he had to be particularly observant of military movements, so he noted down almost anything that might be of significance. This stretch was fairly short, and Hönefoss appeared beneath him. The checkpoint was easy to find, located just beyond a drill field in a shallow valley. The course he was holding carried him directly over the spot, and he called in as usual. Although the temptation to dive again was strong, he resisted it this time. They might possibly subtract points if he tried.

He was nearly finished. Everything had gone remarkably smoothly. How was it going with the others, he wondered. Arild would be well on the way by now. Tore had heard him calling in over A and B, and he would soon reach Dokka. Arild sounded satisfied, so Tore figured that things had worked out well for him so far.

How long had he been in the air? Was it really no

more than forty-five minutes? Tore checked the remaining fuel. Yes, it checked all right. He still had fuel for half an hour. When he arrived at Klöfta, the final checkpoint, he was to return directly to Gardermoen and make two landings, so-called "spot" landings, where the plane is put down within an area marked off on the runway. When you had gotten this far, the rest was pie, he thought. He had nearly forgotten the many landing difficulties he had encountered in the beginning. Now it had become routine, and it was a rare occasion when he messed up a landing and had to go around again and come in once more.

Klöfta was now directly ahead, and Tore concentrated on maneuvering. He had been sloppy this time and flown five degrees off course, but the view from this altitude was so good that he had no trouble locating the red flag. It had been placed on a little hill behind the railroad station and flapped smartly in the wind. A gentle turn brought him directly over the spot. Despite the slightly erroneous navigation, the time checked out nicely, and he radioed the control tower at Gardermoen.

"Gardermoen, Blue 5 over checkpoint F—Foxtrot. Over."

"Roger, Blue 5. Set your course for Gardermoen. You can come in exactly eight minutes from now. Use runway 02, wind is calm at 02 knots from the north. Over."

"Roger," answered Tore. He activated the stopwatch and quickly determined the course he must follow. A rapid calculation in his head gave him his speed, and he was ready for the final approach. He relaxed and settled more comfortably in his seat. The worst was over. It would be exciting to see how well he had managed the trip compared with the many other pilots. One thing was sure, he hadn't loused up a single one of the checkpoints and wouldn't be penalized for that, at least. Now the big questions were how correctly he had calculated the fuel consumption and how well he had done on the observation tests.

Tore's thoughts were interrupted by loud, impressive swearing and a few short groans over the radio. What was going on? Was someone furious at not finding a checkpoint? But Tore thought he detected fear in the voice. And wasn't there something familiar about it?

Before he could ponder the point any longer, he heard Arild's voice speaking clearly and with a slightly ironic overtone over the radio. But the voice shook slightly, too. "Gardermoen, Blue 10 has flown straight into the path of a flock of birds. I heard the impact at various points on the body of the plane. Position thirty seconds from Norefjell. I was flying at 500 feet and am supposedly heading in an easterly direction. Over."

The control tower and the flight director recognized the seriousness of the situation at once. It was no joke to be hit by a bird at 400 to 500 knots per hour. The collision effect would be that of a projectile and could do considerable damage to the plane and its vital parts. If a bird hit the engine intake, it could be sucked straight through and ruin the compressor blades, resulting in engine failure. Now, however, it was not a question of one bird but a whole flock.

"Roger, Blue 10, what do you mean by *'supposedly easterly direction?'* Over."

"I'm not quite sure. I can't see too clearly. My vision is fogging," answered Arild in a strained voice filled with pain.

Tore jumped when he heard the last words. The birds must have hit the windshield and shattered it. At that speed it would be almost impossible to see clearly with the wind blowing directly in one's eyes. And perhaps Arild had been hit by a splinter of glass or a bird . . .

"How high are you now, Blue 10?" It was the tower inquiring.

"It's hard to say, but I pulled up at the same moment I was hit. There's a hole in the cockpit glass directly in front of my head, and I think I've been hit by something because the pain in my eyes is devilish. I can barely see the instruments." The latter was said with a groan.

Tore could tell that Arild was in great pain and that he was using all his willpower not to give in.

"Blue 10, this is the base commander. Bail out and forget the plane!"

"Roger. Don't really have any choice, but it won't be easy."

Tore recalled how he and Arild had often discussed what it would be like to bail out, and Arild had always maintained that there was nothing to it. It was simply a matter of pulling the ejection mechanism and then— poof, you were out and in good shape. But this assumed that one was in top form. Now Arild was injured, and what would happen when he parachuted without being able to see the ground clearly?

Unaware he was doing so, Tore changed course back toward Norefjell, engine at top speed and climbing. Suddenly he realized what he was doing. He was heading for the place Arild had last reported in, and a higher altitude was necessary for him to see further and more clearly. The championship took a back seat. His friend was in danger, and if there was anything he could do, he would certainly try. He could at least determine where Arild would land if he jumped now. It would make it easier for the search party and the helicopter pilot if they knew where Arild was.

Tore sighted swiftly in all directions. He didn't know precisely where Arild was, but from an altitude of 10,000 feet he would locate him pretty fast. He'd better inform the tower of his intentions.

"Gardermoen, this is Blue 5. I am heading for Norefjell, 10,000 feet. I'll try to overtake Blue 10 and follow him when he jumps. Over."

"Roger, Blue 5. We were about to call you. You are the closest of the aircraft. Gardermoen radar will direct you. A helicopter is on the way. Over."

"Roger," replied Tore.

Now another calm voice came over the radio. It was the radar operator who, with the aid of his radar screen, could see the two planes and direct them toward one another and in this way make the search easier for Tore and save valuable time.

"Blue 5 and Blue 10, switch to emergency frequency on the identification channel."

Tore selected the emergency frequency without looking, just as he knew Arild would do. They could locate every instrument and switch in the plane without seeing them, thanks to their intensive training. The radar operator would now receive powerful echoes on his screen and thus be able to identify which plane was Tore's and which was Arild's.

"Blue 5 and Blue 10, I read you clearly now. Blue 5, turn fifteen degrees to the left! Blue 10, maintain your course!"

Tore altered course immediately.

"How's it going, Arild?" he asked.

"I don't know, but the plane is behaving normally at least. My vision is still foggy. I have engaged the automatic pilot and will wait to bail out until you get here."

"Blue 5, you should now have Blue 10 at approximately ten miles, 01 hours."

Tore stared in the direction given by the radar operator, but he couldn't see Arild. He peered eagerly, twisting his head in every direction while he whipped the plane over on its side in order to have a better view downward. Was there something down there, far down there? He thought he saw something reflecting the sunlight. Tore checked the altimeter, which indicated

10,000 feet. If that were a plane down there, it was pretty low.

The radar operator gave Tore a new position that agreed with what he had seen, and without hesitation he plunged into a dive as he simultaneously pulled back the throttle and put out the diving brakes to decrease the speed.

He was just in the vicinity of the city of Hönefoss, and if the plane under him was low, extremely low. . . . He didn't complete the thought. The altimeter spun around crazily, and Tore lost altitude rapidly. He had to pull out of the dive in time, pull out carefully. He was going at dangerously high speed.

"I see you now, Arild. Just keep going, and I'll come up beside you." Tore saw the plane clearly now, but he would place himself at the same altitude as Arild before he said anything further to him. He couldn't risk Arild's panicking if he discovered how low he was. His autopilot must be incorrectly adjusted because it looked as if the plane was steadily losing altitude. Not rapidly, but gradually sinking toward the ground.

Tore admired Arild for being able to fly at all under such conditions, but it was at this point that all his previous experience undoubtedly helped. Arild had demonstrated many times that he had the cool head and steady nerves so necessary to a good pilot. But when he could barely see, it must be like flying in the clouds without instruments.

Tore approached Arild's plane from the rear. It was

flying very low, and a glance at the altimeter told Tore that they couldn't be more than 200 feet above the ground. It looked as if the nose of the plane was heavy and steadily losing altitude.

"OK, Arild, I'm on your left wing. Can you see me?"

"Only like a dark shadow." Arild's voice was a bit desperate, and the half-swallowed groan that followed betrayed the great pain he was in.

"OK. Pull back gently on the stick and give it a little gas. I'll tell you if you're turning or not." Tore spoke quietly, in an everyday tone of voice, while he anxiously watched the top of a hill directly in front of them.

Arild reacted at once to Tore's directions. He pulled on the stick after disengaging the autopilot. The plane began to climb, slowly but surely. Tore kept well away from Arild's wing.

The hilltop passed below them with good clearance, and Tore breathed a sigh of relief. That had been a close call!

"What was my altitude?" asked Arild hesitantly.

"Ah . . . 1,000 feet," lied Tore. He had to avoid panic at all costs. It would make the situation far worse if Arild lost control of himself.

"Gardermoen, Blue 5 is on the wing of Blue 10 now. We are climbing. Position five miles east of Höne-foss, course for Gardermoen," reported Tore. It wasn't really necessary, for the conversation between him and Arild went over the same frequency as the tower's and was monitored from there.

"Roger, Blue 5. Good work! Fly over Blue 10 when he jumps and give us the position. The helicopter is on its way."

"Roger," answered Tore. "Well, Arild, you can get going now. We're at 5,000 feet, so you can flatten out."

"OK. My head's pounding and my eyes are killing me, but I guess I can get out and down in one piece. I can just barely see you on my side, but it is impossible to read the instruments."

"It'll go all right. I'll follow you all the way down and report where you landed. The helicopter'll be along in a minute and pick you up."

"Thanks, Tore, that's great. I actually feel better when I have you on my wing. Read the instruments for me, there's a good guy."

"Speed is 300 knots, you are climbing at 100 feet per minute. You are banked slightly to the left, altitude 5,200 feet, open, smooth terrain under you, so everything looks fine." Tore's voice was so calm one might think it was just a training flight. But inside he was far from calm. He was afraid to think what might happen.

At Gardermoen total emergency had been declared. As soon as the flight director had become aware of the situation, he had pushed the red button, and the helicopter pilots were soon running to the choppers. The radar tower transmitted continuous bearings on the two aircraft, so it would be easy to spot Arild when he bailed out. This simplified the search considerably, and the helicopters, with crew and physician, would fly directly to the drop point. The general, too, had taken up a position in the tower and would follow developments from there. He was engaged in intense conversation with the base commander, who stood bent over a large map. A red cross had been drawn at the planes' location.

"OK, Arild, you can jump! You still have open fields below you, no danger of hitting any trees or getting your feet wet. Forget the plane. It will crash several miles from the nearest house. Good luck!" Tore's voice shook slightly, so he finished up with a joke: "Use your shirttails so you'll have a soft landing!"

"Guess there's nothing else to do. OK, in a couple of seconds I'll be out. Better move or I'll land in your lap." Arild was trying to build courage, too. Tore recognized the effort he was making to remain calm.

Tore slowed down, climbed a little, and maintained a safe distance from Arild. He looked at the fuel indicator and noticed that he didn't have much left in the tank, but it was enough for fifteen minutes' flying. If he figured on five minutes back to Gardermoen, he could circle the jump point for ten minutes and by then the helicopters would have arrived.

Arild was more nervous than he would admit over the radio. His hands shook and his stomach was in a tight knot. He had trimmed the plane as well as he could according to Tore's directions so that it almost flew itself. Several times he shook his head to try to clear his vision, and he felt something wet and sticky running down from his forehead. He wiped his eyes and found his fingers wet afterward. He couldn't see exactly what it was, but it must be blood from the cut in his forehead, which he could trace with his finger. It hurt like fury, and he was sure he would faint when he ejected himself. The parachute fortunately was completely automatic, so it would open at the proper time, but he would have preferred to be able to see the ground approaching. Couldn't he manage to fly home? No. He had to get out!

He began feverishly to go through all that had to be done before he triggered the ejection mechanism. He lowered the seat as far as it would go in order not to be hit when the canopy was shot off. He groped around to check that the parachute was fastened as it ought to be and disconnected the radio wires and the oxygen tube. All clear.

His right hand grasped the ejection handle for the canopy. He clamped his teeth together and tightened every muscle in preparation for what was to come. Quickly he ripped the handle up and waited to hear an explosion and feel the hood sweep past his head.

But nothing happened. He pulled once more with the same result. Had the handle jammed? He squinted tensely and tried in vain to see through the fog surrounding him, but he could only barely see the handle in his right hand. It was all the way up, just where it was supposed to be. The canopy must have jammed during the collision with the bird that had been forced into sharing the cockpit with him. He had heard several thuds, like a drum roll, which meant that several birds had been hit, although only one penetrated the glass. Frantically he connected radio wires to report the situation.

"The hood won't release. I can't get out!" The words were followed by a gulp. Tore had watched Arild continuously. He realized that something must be wrong since such a long time had elapsed from Arild's declaration to jump until the release of the canopy. In fact, no release had taken place.

"Blue 10, this is the base commander. You still have an alternative. You can eject straight through the cockpit hood. Do it! Over."

Yes, it had been done many times before—not in Norway, but by jet pilots from other countries. The pilot receives an additional shock as the seat penetrates the glass, and it is not without considerable danger, but it *was* a way out if one had to evacuate the aircraft.

Arild knew this. Had he any choice?

Desperately he grasped the handle over his head. He shut his eyes and pulled.

The shock he expected didn't come. He was still sitting there. The sweat poured off him. He was soaked inside his flying suit. He pulled and jerked on the handle but with no result. Why didn't the seat move? Had he forgotten to remove the safety pins before takeoff? No, he clearly recalled that the mechanic had removed them for him and put them in the seat pocket. He felt around for them. Yes, they were there. That meant that the ejection mechanism had been damaged in some way. When he had been hit, a number of loose objects had been flung about in the cockpit, and one of them must have been slung with considerable force against the mechanism. Or perhaps something had jammed in a vital spot? At any rate, nothing worked. And what now—would he just stay in the aircraft until the fuel ran out, and then . . .

His morbid thoughts were interrupted by Tore. "Looks like you're in trouble, Arild. I gather the seat is stuck. We're only five minutes from Gardermoen. Do you think you can see well enough to put the plane down there?"

"I sure don't know—I still can't see clearly, but I can distinguish contours and the wings."

Tore's voice was eager. "Arild! Do you remember the time we were training for cloud penetration and my instruments went on the blink? You told me what I should do—how my wings were, speed and altitude, until we came through the cloud cover. We could do this the same way. Want to try?"

The idea gave Arild new hope. Now he clung to Tore.

There was no comment from Gardermoen. Everyone was following the conversation between the two pilots closely. No one dared to interrupt with suggestions or remarks. This must be decided between the two of them—the one in a desperate situation but still clinging to a slight hope, the other in the process of encouraging his friend and convincing him to attempt something that would be fatal if it failed.

Arild's answer was not long in coming.

"OK, Tore, get going! I don't know if it will work, but I'll do my best." His voice held renewed life. He was tense, but at the same time in balance and ready for a tremendous effort. The pain had subsided a bit, but his vision was still clouded.

"Great, Arild! I'm positioned on your right side now. Your speed is 300 knots, so keep a steady throttle. We have to turn 30 degrees to the left. . . . Go ahead!"

Arild moved the stick carefully to the left and felt the plane bank. He counted the seconds, and five seconds before the time was up he rolled out carefully. He could glimpse the plane beside him and saw that the wings were in proper position.

"Blue 5 from Gardermoen. Understand that you are bringing Blue 10 to the base and will attempt landing. All clear here. How much fuel do you have? Over."

Tore had a sinking feeling. Fuel—he'd forgotten that. Perhaps he hadn't enough. Then it would be *he* who would have to bail out, and both planes would be lost. But that didn't solve the problem. What about Arild?

"Yeah, how much do you have left, Tore?" Arild felt defeat creep closer. If Tore didn't have enough, *he* was finished.

"No sweat. I have enough for ten minutes, and we'll be there six minutes from now."

Tore had added a couple of minutes. Actually he had no more than seven minutes, approximately, but he wasn't going to tell Arild.

"Your position is good, Arild. Just ease a couple of degrees to the right. We'll go down to 3,000 feet so we have a long, shallow glide path."

"OK. Just give the orders, Tore. I'll follow as well as I can." He depended on Tore—he *had* to depend on Tore now. But things looked pretty black—he'd have to admit that.

Tore managed to turn the two planes so that their course lay directly toward the base. He wanted to avoid too many corrections to the side; Arild would have his hands full following the descent and holding the correct speed. The really dangerous phase would come as they approached the runway and he set the plane down on the ground. If he hit too hard, or lost control because of insufficient speed, he would wreck both himself and the plane. It was true that the K tolerated fairly hard landings, but . . . he didn't feel particularly hopeful.

"Reduce your speed a little, Arild. You're gliding ahead of me." The calm in Tore's voice was false; he was trying to reassure both Arild and himself. Actually he was on the verge of losing his own control.

Arild reacted by drawing back ever so little on the throttle and trimming the nose of the plane up a bit.

"Great. We're holding 500 feet descent per minute, and that ought to be about right."

Tore hadn't considered whether he ought to land together with Arild or if he ought to follow him down as far as possible and then go around again and land afterward. The base lay in a direct line from the nose of Arild's plane. He maintained his own position slightly to the right of the runway.

There was utter silence on the radio. The other pilots must have been directed over another frequency in order that Tore and Arild might use their own with no danger of interruption.

"How's it going? See anything in front of you?"

"Well . . . the headache's less, and I think I can distinguish something or other out there. I get a little of the outline of your plane, but I can't read my instruments."

Tore had an idea and called in to the tower: "Turn on the runway lights full blast, and direct a few vehicles to either side of the runway, ready to fire red and green signal flares! Over." Tore never gave a thought to the fact that he was giving orders to the base commander himself.

The general and the colonel looked at one another and nodded. Why hadn't they thought of this themselves!

"Direct the entire squadron to assume positions along the runway, first driving to the depot for issue of every signal pistol in stock, plus ammunition! We've got about four minutes." The general's voice was authoritative. The flight director was already in contact with the squadron room and gave his orders.

"Blue 5, orders completed." The general smiled briefly as he reported over the radio.

"Can you see anything more now, Arild?" asked Tore.

"I'm not sure, but I think I can discern some lights

in front of the nose." Arild's voice was brighter now. The hope of seeing more clearly had improved his mood somewhat. His eyes still hurt, but the pain was no longer so intense.

"Good, Arild. We have about four minutes left and are lying pretty far away, so you certainly ought to be able to see the lights and signal flares as we approach." Tore was relieved at Arild's reply. If he were able to steer him in now to the landing strip and keep an eye on the altitude and speed, Arild would certainly be able to set the plane down even if it were a hard landing.

"Maintain your position—you're doing great! Wings are horizontal, and your altitude is 2,000 feet. When we reach 1,500 feet, we'll alter the angle so we have a flatter approach."

"OK." Arild seemed almost cheerful now.

"You'd better land without flaps."

Arild understood the reason for this. There is always the danger of a jet aircraft losing all life under the wings if the speed is too little and the pilot is using full flaps. Not only that, but Arild couldn't be sure that he would react quickly enough to Tore's orders if it suddenly were necessary for him to give it full power and thereby ruin the entire approach! His fuel capacity was sufficient for another round, but . . . he undoubtedly had more fuel than Tore since he had interrupted the navigation trial earlier.

Through binoculars the men in the tower watched the two pilots approach the base in a glide. The general and the base commander nodded in agreement as they listened to Tore's orders.

Four fire engines were stationed on the runway, two on either side, prepared for emergency assistance. The ambulance, carrying Dr. Wide, was parked halfway down the left side of the runway. A number of observers had gathered on the roof of the base restaurant. The rumor had spread rapidly that a critical situation had developed. The pilots who had not been ordered to man the runway with flare guns were also on the roof. They could easily put themselves in Arild's shoes, and they admired his courage.

Three planes that had completed the navigation flight circled the base waiting for clearance to land. The control tower took no chances in clearing them for landing now; they might, for example, puncture while landing and block the runway for the other two planes.

Tore darted anxious glances toward the fuel indicator, which now measured dangerously low, about two minutes left. But now it was only a question of Arild. Afterward he would manage to get down somehow.

"Lower your nose a bit, Arild; we're a bit too high. Enough. That's fine. Hold it that way for a while. . . . Extend fourteen degrees of flaps now. I think that ought to do the trick."

"OK, flaps down a notch. Are they out?"

"Yeah, great. We won't use speed brakes—we've got to maintain speed as long as possible."

"Agreed," replied Arild. He followed Tore's directions without hesitation.

"Get ready, Arild. Wheels have to come out—*now!*"

Arild put his hand on the gear handle and pulled. He felt the welcome vibration as the wheels dropped out of the wheel wells and descended. Immediately afterward he felt a slight shock pass through the plane, an indication that they were down and locked. He tried to distinguish the instruments that indicated the wheels' position, but was unable to see them clearly.

"Your wheels are out and locked," Tore said. He was impressed with how well Arild was handling the plane. With the intense pain and partial loss of vision, it was an outstanding performance to be able to fly at all. A person with several thousand flying hours behind him ought to be familiar with a plane's slightest movement and know the cockpit inside and out, but even so . . .

"Your speed is just a bit low, Arild. An inch of throttle and it ought to be all right. Your wheels drag heavily, you know."

Arild had forgotten to give it a little more gas as the wheels dropped. If he had been able to see clearly, the speedometer would have indicated the danger. He gave it the necessary inch.

"That'll do it. We now have twenty knots' excess speed. If we maintain it past the end of the runway, there should be no danger of the plane's stalling too soon."

"Roger," answered Arild.

Tore continued in an imperturbed voice. Arild must not sense how afraid he was. They were beginning the final, deadly serious phase now. "I'll be giving you slight corrections all the way in from now on, and when I tell you to cut the motor, you must trust me and do it. If you get a nasty bump on the ground, it won't matter so much."

"I can take that all right. Just keep talking, pal— I'll do whatever you say. As a matter of fact, I can make out the runway lights more clearly now. Try a rocket and I'll see if I can catch sight of it."

Tore was about to request exactly the same thing, and he saw that the flight leader had already reacted. At the end of a runway a red signal rocket soared.

The flight director was in radio contact with one of the jeeps along the runway, and the driver had passed on the order to one of the pilots who stood waiting with a pistol. Many of the pilots armed with signal pistols and ammunition had now taken their positions at regular intervals from the end of the strip down to the middle of the runway.

Arild peered eagerly ahead. Yes, right in front of the nose of the plane he saw a pale red light climbing skyward!

"I can see it!" he babbled excitedly into the radio. His joy at having dependable landmarks made him forget the pain and the situation for a moment. "It wasn't completely clear, but at least I could distinguish the light," he added more matter of factly.

"Terrific, Arild! We've got this thing in the bag for sure. When we approach the edge of the runway, everyone can fire his pistol and you can land in the middle of some beautiful fireworks." Tore felt more optimistic. "OK, Arild, we're down to 800 feet. With the speed we're holding now, you will reach the edge of the runway at approximately 100 feet. Emergency cables are erected at the other end. If you overrun the edge after landing, just keep going. It's good and firm there. The worst that could happen is that you will break your supports. Are you strapped in tightly?"

"Tight as a drum. I can't move."

"Gardermoen, you can see us now. I am not landing with Blue 10." Tore had made his decision; it was too dangerous to land in close formation when there was a risk of Arild's veering to the side. The fuel indicator showed zero, but he hoped it was not correctly adjusted. At least the motor was still running smoothly.

"Roger. Whatever you say, Blue 5. You can come in after Blue 10 is safely down."

Tore acknowledged and hoped he would be able to do just that.

"We'll cut down five knots, Arild. We're a hair too high . . . good, now it's right . . . 500 feet left. It's going great. Remember, you're going to land like butter." He thought he'd better toss out a little joke for mutual encouragement. His stomach was painfully knotted, and his hands shook. How must Arild be feeling? He was wringing wet himself and had to keep wiping away the perspiration that ran down into his eyes.

The approach looked ideal. The angle was good and the speed as calculated. If only Arild's nerves held out until he had cut the motor just above the runway! But Arild had the steadiest nerves of anyone in the squadron, so there was little danger that he would panic in the final, decisive moment.

"We are now at 200 feet and approaching the edge of the runway. Are you ready?"

"Roger." Arild's voice was tense. He strained to see through the fog that still hung before his eyes. The ache in his head had returned, and he had to clench his teeth to keep from crying out.

"Get set now, Arild—we are over the edge. Pull carefully on the stick, a little less gas! Good! You are ten feet above the runway . . . this is going perfectly . . . cut the motor! Good luck!" Tore could do nothing further for Arild now. The rest fate would decide—fate and Arild's skill as a pilot.

Tore shoved the throttle all the way forward and sighed with relief as the motor responded. At the same time he pulled the plane up and gained altitude each second. If the motor failed now from lack of fuel, he would still be able to set the plane down in a glide. He now had sufficient height.

Arild had waited for the order to cut the motor with pounding heart. He saw several signal flares shoot up beside the plane. They resembled small, dull glimmers through the fog. With a dead motor he felt how the plane began to shake and approach the stall. If the altitude above the landing strip was correct, the plane would drop the remaining feet and he would feel the main gear hit the concrete. He clenched his teeth, braced his feet against the rudder pedals, and waited for whatever was to come—either a crash or a roll down the runway.

110

In the tower and on the roof of the nearby building, everyone held his breath.

A powerful shock went through the plane, then another. The nose wheel banged down on the concrete. If the plane were now in a line with the runway, it would go by itself until it came to a stop. Arild could do nothing about directing it with the aid of the brakes. He couldn't see the edge of the runway. He'd either make it or he wouldn't. He crumpled down into the seat. At least he was on the ground again.

Suddenly he heard a voice over the radio: "Release the drag chute, Blue 10!" It was the base commander who shouted as he saw the plane was about to go off the runway.

Arild reacted instantaneously. His hand located the release without hesitation.

Suddenly he was thrown forward, and everything was blacked out.

On the runway, the plane suddenly changed direction and cut off to the side. Thanks to the drag chute, the speed was not excessive, but the nose wheel hit the concrete edge and broke off, causing the nose section to hit the ground and plow a deep furrow in the earth. As a result of the abrupt stop the rear end of the plane was lifted, and for a moment it looked as if the plane would flip over on its back. It did not, however, but fell heavily to one side. The wing broke and the aircraft lay still.

If the plane had landed on its back, things would

have looked bad for Arild. He would have been so firmly imprisoned that he would have had to be cut loose, and the plane might have caught fire.

Four fire engines with screaming sirens tore down the runway, and the firemen jumped out with hoses at the ready. Arild heard the noise dimly in the distance, but didn't understand what it was. Now he only wanted to sleep—sleep for days.

The ambulance was the next to reach the plane, and Dr. Wide jumped out before it had come to a full stop. He had no idea what he would find in the cockpit, but he was filled with misgivings. One of the firemen arrived with an ax and began chopping on the hood of the cockpit. The release mechanism on the outside was also out of order. It wasn't long before the hood was freed, and Dr. Wide bent over Arild, who hung in the harness. He loosened the straps and gestured to the fireman to help him free Arild from the seat. Carefully they lifted him out and placed him on a stretcher. Dr. Wide unbuckled the parachute from Arild, spread a blanket over him, and examined him quickly and superficially before he was driven to the hospital. Wide stared at the bloody face and swollen eyes, which opened suddenly. Arild attempted to say something, but was unable to get a word out.

"Relax, Arild! You're down safely. I'll give you something to make you sleep, and you can sleep for two weeks if you want to."

A weak smile appeared on Arild's lips, and Wide heard him whisper, "Tore, is he . . ."

Wide squinted toward the runway and saw a plane coming in for landing.

"He's coming in now, Arild. Everything's fine."

Arild sighed, and his body grew limp. He had passed out.

Tore had almost shouted aloud when he saw Arild's plane rush toward the edge of the runway and then lurch forward almost on its nose. It was a ghastly sight. At any moment he expected to hear a violent explosion and see the plane engulfed in flames. But he had no time to devote any more than passing notice to the plane because he suddenly saw the red light warning him that he had only a few seconds before his engine conked out.

The extra power he had gained when gunning the engine after leaving Arild had given him sufficient altitude to cope with engine failure.

"Gardermoen, Blue 5. My engine is out. I'm at 5,000 feet, approaching from the south. Over."

This came as no surprise to the flight leader. He had checked the amount of fuel Tore ought to have and determined that engine failure could occur at any time.

"There's a cold-blooded kid. What if . . ." The general did not complete his sentence. Had Tore's plane quit . . .

Tore made all the necessary checks as he went into a long, descending left turn toward the base. At least this would be a lot simpler than the time he had no wheels out.

When he was low enough, he flipped the wheel switch, and a comforting little thud told him they were down and locked.

Tore flew automatically. The plane swung into its final leg. He wasn't the least bit nervous, just extremely tired. The runway lay invitingly ahead of him, and he'd have to be very unlucky not to hit it, wide and long as it was. It was as if he were making a practice emergency landing. Everything was carried out with flair and precision, and it was difficult to tell if the aircraft had an engine or not.

Tore glided down the finale and was soon over the edge of the runway. His speed was a bit excessive, but he had plenty of runway ahead of him, so it made no difference.

The plane took the ground at about the first one-third marker. Tore released the drag chute, and the plane rolled gently down the strip and came to a full stop just at the end.

"OK, Blue 5. Well done!" It was the general speaking into the microphone, expressing the opinion of everyone.

"Thanks, General."

Tore sank back in his seat with relief. Then came the reaction. His hands began to shake violently, and he knew he would not be able to get out of the cockpit under his own steam. He'd better wait until the tractor came to pull him in to the hangar.

The planes that had been kept aloft over the base now came in for landings and rolled slowly past him as they waved their congratulations.

A yellow tractor came full speed from the squadron area and headed for Tore. He could see Lie waving. Tore loosened his straps and hauled himself up. The tractor stopped, and Lie hopped up on the wing to give Tore a hand. He was grateful for the help, as his legs barely supported him. He slipped gently down on the ground and did a few awkward knee bends to get the stiffness out of his body.

Lie was one huge smile. "If I'd known you were going to need more gas, I'd have put more in the tank."

"Yeah, I could have used a drop or two more, but you gave me just barely enough." Tore found he had enough energy for a joke. The tough part of the job was finished.

In the midst of the confusion Tore had forgotten his mascot. Now he crawled stiffly up on the wing again and returned with the little troll dangling from one hand. "Thanks a lot; it was a pleasant surprise to find this in the cockpit. It saved my life today, perhaps Arild's, too," he said. "Anyway, thanks for lending it to me."

He offered the mascot to Lie. "No, keep it. You've certainly earned it. It brought you better luck than it ever brought me."

Tore once again climbed laboriously back up on the wing and hung the troll in its place on the instrument panel. He gave it a little push, and it seemed to smile at him.

It took only a moment to attach the tractor to the nose wheel of the plane, and they were on their way to the hangar.

With his parachute slung over his shoulder, Tore walked toward the squadron room.

He was greeted with loud shouts, and all the pilots came over to shake his hand and congratulate him. Tore was almost embarrassed at all the fuss and said that he had done no more than any one of them would have done in a similar situation. "Don't forget Arild," he added. "It was he who did the big job."

"Yes, in a way," admitted one of the pilots. "But he never could have done it alone."

Then the talk began again: "How's Arild? Was the plane badly damaged? Is there any danger to his vision? Was there a hole in the cockpit?" The questions rained down over Tore, who knew less than they did.

One of the pilots called the hospital to get more information about Arild. The others could tell by his smile that the news was good. He put down the receiver and reported: "Doctor Wide says he had a few small splinters in his eyes and they have been removed. There is no danger to his vision, and he'll soon be in shape again."

That was good news indeed. Arild was greatly admired among his friends in the squadron. Tore sank into a chair and sighed contentedly. Boy, was he tired and wet! He'd better see about a shower. No one had time to talk about the Norwegian championship, and he himself no longer cared about the outcome. Squadron 666 could not be in the running any more since two of them had dropped out of the race. He had completed the actual course but had not had time for the two spot landings at the finish.

Tore rose and walked out to the dressing room to shower and change. He met Major Halse coming out.

"Heard you had a little trouble," he said with a smile. He clasped Tore's hand and shook it. "An outstanding performance. It must have been a tough proposition."

"Thanks, Major. But it wasn't I who had the toughest part. Poor Arild really had to sweat it out."

"Undoubtedly. A courageous job. I doubt that many others could have done it. But your following him in without so much as one extra drop of fuel was . . . well, that wasn't too bad either! We in the squadron are extremely proud of both of you."

"Thank you, Major. But I only did my duty."

"Not only your duty. I'd say it was also a real test of friendship—test passed with flying colors! Well, hurry up and get changed—the general would like a word with you."

Tore's head was spinning with all the hullabaloo. It wasn't *that* much to make a fuss over. The shower felt good. He was stiff and tired in every muscle and only wanted to go to the barracks and hit the sack. Oh yes, the general. He had never spoken with a general before. Ought he to say, "Yes, General," and "No, General," and stand stiffly at attention as if he had swallowed a ruler?

The first thing Tore saw when he opened the door to the lounge was the general in conversation with Major Halse. Everyone turned as Tore entered. He saluted, but the general came over to him informally and grasped both his hands.

"What I witnessed today was an unforgettable experience for me. You did a fine job: a well-thought-out, brave, and highly competent job."

"But, General . . ." began Tore, but he was interrupted by the general.

"Yes, yes—I am aware that it was Second Lieutenant Nansen flying the other plane, but without your cold-headedness and effective orders, he would never have been able to carry out your instructions."

The general began fumbling in his pockets and finally found what he was looking for. He held it up for all to see.

"This is an old gilded squadron insignia. It is unusual for a jet pilot to be decorated, but it is my wish that Sergeant Bö be honored with this insignia," he said with a warm smile. "I cannot do this officially on behalf of the Air Force, so I suggest that we all give him this for his demonstration of bravery, ability, and loyalty toward a friend."

The general pinned the squadron insignia on Tore's chest amidst enthusiastic applause. Tore did not know what to say. He found the whole affair extremely embarrassing and only managed a scarcely audible "thank you."

The pilots came over to Tore, and each in turn shook hands with him. When it was finished, he dropped into a chair as his legs could barely support him. He looked at his right hand, feeling that it must be crushed flat, but it was only a bit redder than usual.

The talk was lively and noisy until someone began shushing the others. The general had raised his hand and was waving a large sheet of paper.

"All right, pilots. I have the results of today's competition. You all had almost forgotten about it, eh?"

There was a sudden silence, and the pilots chuckled. The general wasn't a bad fellow, in spite of all that gold braid.

Tore relaxed. They had no chance of winning the squadron trophy after Arild had had to drop out. Knutsen had come over to Tore and dropped into an empty chair at his side. Tore hadn't had time to ask either him or the major how they had made out.

"I see from all the notations on this sheet that one name is missing," began the general. "And you all know who it is. It is a great pity, since he would have only had to complete the run with a result below average in order for his squadron to win. I feel I ought to mention this. Not that it detracts from the efforts of the triumphant squadron, but an undeserved accident ought not to take away the opportunity to be mentioned with honor." The general put on his glasses in order to read better.

"Let us now turn to this list. We see that every single one of the pilots scored a 'grand slam' in observation tests in the field. This is extremely important for a jet pilot—to have his eyes open and be able to discriminate between important and insignificant things."

The general paused, and Tore whispered to Knutsen, "How's Arild?"

"Great. I just called," Knutsen whispered back.

The general cleared his throat and continued. "I now have the privilege of declaring that the Norwegian Championship in Navigation Flying has been won by the country's northernmost squadron, namely Squadron 366 from Bardufoss."

Everyone clapped, and the four pilots from Squadron 366 smiled blissfully. When the crowd had quieted down, the general continued.

"Next comes the individual championship. I can only say that according to the impression I received during today's flying, I am not in the least surprised that he was the winner."

Tore felt Knutsen's elbow in his side. He had only half listened, without really registering what the general was saying. Half in a daze he heard the general continue.

"I know that every one of you will join me in a squadron cheer for the champion of today's competition." Tore still could not understand why everyone was staring at him and smiling broadly. "Namely," continued the general, "our newly decorated young pilot, Sergeant Tore Bö!"

The yells and the squadron cheer were deafening. If the roof had not been concrete, it would have risen a couple of inches.

Knutsen leaned over to him. "Congratulations, Tore. I've always had a lot of faith in you. You can fly *my* wing any time."

Tore greatly appreciated his words. He was still only a sergeant, and he had had a lot of luck today. Knutsen had a great deal to teach him, and such a compliment from one of the oldest pilots gave him a warm feeling.

The general had not finished and requested silence. He read aloud the remainder of the list, and it turned out that Major Halse had been number five and Knutsen number seven.

Halse had come over to them, and together they discussed the results. "It went extremely well," said the major. "If we had had Arild with us this time, we would have won. But so what—there's always another bus coming along. We'll catch it next year."

Tore was still in a dreamlike state. He could not quite believe that he had beaten all of these experienced pilots.

"Come on, let's go over and say hello to Arild," said Halse suddenly. "Dr. Wide said it was all right if we visited him, but no one else should for the time being."

Tore jumped to his feet and again felt his sore muscles. But his only thought was to visit Arild.

They piled into the jeep, and the major drove them to the hospital. It was quite a change from the way Arild took the curves with a screaming of tires, thought Tore.

Dr. Wide showed them to the patient's room. Arild

sat in bed supported by pillows. In his lap was a tray of food, and it didn't look as if his appetite had been affected.

"Who is it?" he inquired.

"How's the boy, Arild? We had to see how they were treating you."

"Is it *you*, Tore? Come on over here so I can shake your hand."

Tore walked over to the bed. He found he had to place his own hand in Arild's.

"I can't see too well yet, but the doc says my eyeballs will be in shape in a few days. Seems he had to pluck out a few feathers."

The others approached the bed and greeted Arild warmly, their words full of praise for what he had done.

"Drop it," said Arild, and squinted at them. "The credit belongs to Tore. He maneuvered the plane—I supplied the automation."

They perched on the edge of the bed and told him about the results of the championship.

"Tore won, sure," said Arild. "Who else? He even had time to be my babysitter during the whole merry-go-round! But if I'd been able to complete the course, you'd have had to fight for your points."

Then the major told him that Tore had run out of fuel just after Arild had landed.

Arild frowned. "Is that true, Tore?"

Tore had to admit that it was.

"I've never heard of such a thing. Why didn't you tell me?"

"It wouldn't have helped much. I figured you had more than enough to think about without adding my problems to your own."

"True enough. You saved my life, you jerk. How can I pay you back?"

"Nuts, that wasn't such a big deal. Besides," added Tore, "I don't like losing a pal when I've just found him."

Arild nodded. "Agreed," he said. "Very logical. My feeling exactly."

The major cleared his throat. "You two undoubtedly have plenty to talk about, so Knutsen and I'll be on our way. Take it easy, Arild, and get back on your feet in a hurry. We need you in the squadron, you know."

"Thanks for coming, Major. You, too, Knutsen. Sorry I left some unfinished business today."

"Oh, stow it. Next time we'll take them in such style they won't know what hit them!"

The two friends were left alone. Sergeant Bö and Second Lieutenant Arild Nansen discussed various flights that were coming up and were so absorbed in their subject that they didn't notice Dr. Wide when he stuck his head in the door to see about Arild. Wide closed it again with a smile. Let them talk in peace; they had experienced enough today to fill a book.